COMMUNITY CARE IN BRITAIN: VARIATIONS ON A THEME

David J Hunter and Gerald Wistow

King Edward's Hospital Fund for London

© King Edward's Hospital Fund for London 1987
Typeset by Tradespools Ltd, Frome, Somerset
Printed and bound in England by Redwood Burn Ltd,
Trowbridge, Wiltshire

ISBN 0 900889 92 6

King's Fund Publishing Office
2 St Andrew's Place
London NW1 4LB

PREFACE

This book originated in our growing appreciation that there are significant differences between England, Scotland and Wales in the organisation and provision of health and social care. At the same time it became clear that the literature charting these differences was both sparse and widely scattered. The purpose of our collaboration has been to explore more systematically and, where possible, account for the nature and extent of diversity in this field, especially with reference to community care policies. In particular we have been motivated by two concerns: first, an interest in establishing how far policy diversity can be accommodated within an apparently unitary political system; second, a belief that policy-makers and practitioners might profit from the realisation that constraints evident in one country may not be universal. Community care provides a useful opportunity to pursue these concerns given the varying commitment to the policy initiative within England, Scotland and Wales.

In undertaking what was, in the first instance, a mapping exercise, we have drawn upon a wide range of literature as well as empirical work in which we have both been previously involved. These sources were supplemented by interviews conducted over the summer of 1985 with officials in the Scottish and Welsh Offices. We wish to express our gratitude to all the officials who gave so generously of their time both in interviews and in commenting on an earlier draft of our report. In addition, our understanding of this field has been deepened over a longer period of time by numerous discussions in health and local authorities within each of the three countries as well as through contacts with voluntary organisations and central government departments. The conventions under which such research is conducted preclude us from acknowledging the contribution of particular individuals. However, and especially in view of the pressures of time under which public officials and others have to work, we wish to record our debt for the readiness with which they have assisted our research. We should also like to thank David Goda for commenting on the section on service and resource profiles in Chapter 4, and our secretaries, Lorraine Gibb and Janet Tiernan, for typing successive drafts. In addition, uncomplainingly and under great pressure, Lorraine undertook all word processing in the preparation of a final text for publication. Finally, we wish to thank the Royal Institute of

3

Public Administration for providing such congenial surroundings in which to pursue, on numerous occasions, our collaborative work. The views expressed herein are, of course, our own and do not necessarily represent those of the individuals who assisted us.

David J Hunter
University of Aberdeen and King's Fund Institute, London
Gerald Wistow
Loughborough University of Technology
September 1986

CONTENTS

TABLES

FIGURES

Chapter 1
INTRODUCTION

Studies of central-local relationships have become plentiful in recent years, many of them carried out under the aegis of the research initiative promoted by the then Social Science Research Council (SSRC) in the late 1970s (Social Science Research Council 1979; Jones 1980; Goldsmith 1986b). Surprisingly little work has been carried out, however, on what we term 'centre-centre relationships' within the United Kingdom. By this, we mean the nature, direction and outcome of relationships between London, Edinburgh, Cardiff and Belfast. As Madgwick and Rose (1982, page 3) have noted:

> ... studies of 'British' politics concentrate upon the politics of the largest single nation, England... The relationships between Westminster and its constituent national parts are usually neglected, even though they are very different from relationships between local government and central government departments ...

Our concern in this study of the evolution of community care policy in Britain focuses upon two manifestations of diversity: that which is a feature of centre-centre relations, and that which is a feature of policy formulation and its subsequent implementation. Taken together they are useful navigational aids in an exploration of the complexity underlying a policy initiative that at one level has all the appearance of being uniform in its conception while at another is multi-faceted and variegated in both its form and realisation.

In the field of health and social services the absence of intra-UK research is often remarked upon but relatively little work has been undertaken to follow up an initial ground clearing exercise sponsored by the then SSRC some years ago (Williamson and Room 1983). Studies of policy-making and management in health and related fields have generally been confined to the English context even when professing to embrace Britain or the UK. Indeed, the existence of quite distinct and separate arrangements for the administration of health and social care within the constituent parts of the UK has received no more than a fleeting acknowledgement. Scarcely any attention has been devoted to the systematic comparison of those arrangements and especially to whether variations in structure and process are associated with variations in policy outputs (Hunter 1982; 1983b). One of us (Hunter 1982, 1983b) has attempted to describe the different structures of the NHS in each of the constituent parts of the UK as a prelude to further analysis of the differences in an attempt to determine their significance in a variety of policy issues. The other has started from the other end of the policy process and charted differences in policy and service outputs to be found across Britain in the field of mental handicap (Wistow 1985).

Mapping administrative permutations can be no more than a small first step in the task of investigating their implications for health policy delivery. The NHS may *look* different in the constituent parts of the UK but *is* it different in practice? In this introductory section we explore the reasons for believing that intra-UK comparative work in health and social care is desirable and set out the approach we adopted in this study. In the case of health it may be that the terminology of a '*National* Health Service' itself helps to obscure the reality of four health services, administered by separate departments and accountable to different political masters each with an independent voice in Cabinet. The persistence of such variations (a further set of variations is evident *within* each of the four countries but we are not concerned with these here) gives the lie to the commonly held assumption that there exists only one NHS which is highly centralised and monolithic in its operation. The reality is infinitely more complex.

To the extent that intra-UK distinctions are made, the DHSS in England is usually accorded the status of 'lead' department for health matters. The conventional wisdom is that the Scottish, Welsh and Northern Ireland Offices have a predominantly reactive role, taking their cue from the DHSS rather than developing independent initiatives of their own. The ascription of policy leadership to the DHSS is only a particular example of the leadership role more generally associated with the functional departments in Whitehall – health is not the odd man out in this respect (Keating and Midwinter 1983, page 208). This, in turn, is derived from the highly centralised constitutional and political framework within which the territorial departments operate (Kellas and Madgwick 1982, page 21). Indeed Owen (1979) has described the UK as the most centralised state of all the Western democracies. If political heterogeneity is now more widely recognised following the Nationalist successes of the 1960s and 1970s in Scotland and Wales, the Whitehall-Westminster axis is still seen to impose a broad measure of policy homogeneity. In a unitary state, a unitary policy framework prevails which imposes strict limits on the extent to which divergence in substantive policy is possible or permissible. Such, at least, is the conventional wisdom.

It is not surprising, therefore, to find policy analysts concluding that 'the pressures for the alignment of policy within the Whitehall framework are considerable' (Keating and Midwinter 1983, page 25).

Similarly, Kellas (1975, page 209) has suggested that in Britain diversity in policy-making between different parts of the country is only tolerable if it concerns means rather than ends. As he accepts, such a distinction is not always easy to draw in particular cases. Equally, the degree of 'action space' has appeared to vary between, and even within, policy fields: pressures for conformity being particularly strong in the case of economic policy but perhaps less substantial in the social policy field. The distinctive history and tradition of the Scottish education system may be cited in support of the latter point, as may the reorganisation of social work services in Scotland in advance of, and at variance with, the pattern adopted in England and Wales (Cooper 1983; Smith 1983). Even so, Parry's (1981, page 35) review of the scope for autonomy in Scottish social policy suggested that social work reorganisation was an exceptional case which 'relied on contingencies which seldom recur'. Education is more mixed: some fundamental issues of education policy, such as introducing comprehensive education and raising the school leaving age, are common to all three countries (Kellas 1979, page 17) while others, such as the examination system and aspects of higher education, differ sharply.

At first sight, the scope for autonomy in Welsh policy-making seems even more restricted than in Scotland. Compared with the Scottish Office, its Welsh counterpart is both smaller in scope and size (with about a quarter the staff) and younger. While 1985 marked the centenary of the Scottish Office, it was only in that year the Welsh Office 'attained its majority' having been part of the Whitehall Ministry of Housing and Local Government until as recently as 1964. Moreover, responsibility for health and personal social services was not devolved from the DHSS until 1969 and 1971 respectively, while the Home Office remains responsible for law and order in the Principality. Indeed, the existence of a common legal system for England and Wales contrasts sharply with the distinctive legal traditions and institutions in Scotland which give rise to so much of the need for separate Scottish legislation. By contrast, separate Welsh legislation is rare.

Historically, therefore, the administrative and legal integration of Wales with England has been, and in some respects remains, closer and more longstanding than that of Scotland. The Welsh language continues to be a feature which distinguishes Wales as the only genuinely bilingual constituent of the United Kingdom. However, while it is occasionally a significant factor in the administration and delivery of health and welfare services, it raises few, if any, strategic issues which differentiate policy-making for such services from those elsewhere.

11

Generally speaking there is widespread agreement among commentators with Keating and Midwinter's (1983, page 26) view that 'greater degrees of autonomy are likely over organisational issues of administrative process than functional policies' within Scotland and Wales. The established view seems to be that, insofar as the prevailing political and policy processes permit intra-UK variations, they operate for the most part at the level of administrative structure and process (that is, means) rather than at the level of basic service objectives (that is, ends). As a result, and as Kellas and Madgwick (1982, page 29) conclude from their review of the Scottish and Welsh Offices, 'for most of the time (those) two Offices are engaged in the humdrum business of implementing policies made elsewhere and introducing modest variations where they can to suit the conditions, needs and idiosyncracies of the two countries'. It is also the case that the Welsh and Scottish Offices operate differently from each other as well as from Whitehall departments.

Despite all that has been written and said on the subject, the paradox of considerable policy diversity within a unitary state remains a curious anomaly. It is, moreover, by no means necessarily confined to policy means rather than ends. After all, where does one begin and the other end? There is a burgeoning literature on the subject of policy formation and implementation which shares the view that these are not discrete processes but are highly interrelated. Is it possible to be certain that the particular means employed, or not employed, to implement a policy have no impact on the shape of the policy or on its ultimate success or failure? Another dimension of the interaction between means and ends is that differences in means may be indicative of the extent to which the same policy goals effectively have divergent meanings and priorities within the British social care system. We hope to shed light on some of these issues in the study of one major policy initiative – community care. In doing so, we share Lipsky's (1978, page 397) view that 'there are many contexts in which the latitude of those charged with carrying out policy is so substantial that studies of implementation should be turned on their heads. In these cases policy is effectively "made" by the people who implement it'. Policy analysts, therefore, no longer subscribe to a simple division between policy and implementation – the two activities are intertwined. Thus the notion that policy is made by the centre to be implemented faithfully at local level cannot pass without challenge. As Ham and Hill (1984) argue, implementation cannot be separated from policy-making. This argument applies with equal force to centre-centre as to central-local relations.

The theories of Lipsky and others have found their way into studies of central-local government relations within both England and

Scotland. But there are really two sets of relationships at work within Britain and the traffic is by no means all one way (that is, emanating from Whitehall). It is necessary to distinguish between central-local relations *within* each of the constituent parts of the UK, and the centre-centre relations *between* them. While the former have been subjected to considerable scrutiny (especially in England) the latter, as we have already pointed out, have been virtually neglected.

In our study of health and social care in Britain and its administration we are concerned both with how far the DHSS acts as the lead department for policy-making in this field and also with the extent to which 'administrative creativity' (Parry 1981, page 3) sits alongside policy conformity. Taking community care for dependent groups as a case example of an established policy initiative across Britain we suggest that the twin notions of policy uniformity and the lead department are neither simple nor self-evident. Considerable variation in both policy and practice, if looked for, can be found. If nothing else, our study demonstrates the heterogeneity of experience in community care and the limitations of studying health and social services in England as if they were typical of, if not synonymous with, practice in the rest of Britain.

A case study approach has strengths and limitations. Its chief appeal lies in the depth to which it is possible to go to understand a particular policy process. Its chief limitation lies in too readily making generalisations from the particular. It is our contention that generalisations may not be helpful in understanding practice and, indeed, may obscure important differences. At the most general level, community care has all the appearance of a uniform policy as set out in numerous official reports published singly or jointly by the three central health departments. Yet marked differences exist in both the meaning and degree of emphasis that have been accorded to this goal and also in the instruments associated with its implementation. We believe it is only through a more detailed review of a particular policy issue that many of the nuances of centre-centre relationships and policy autonomy begin to become evident.

The boundaries of our case study have had to be more closely delimited than might ideally have been the case. We have, for example, as may have already been noted, excluded Northern Ireland from our analysis because it shares fewer common features than the mainland territories. In particular, the administrative integration at all levels of the Province's health and personal social services provides a quite different structural context, the consequences of which merit – and have already been the subject of – separate enquiry (for example, Royal Commission on the National Health Service 1978; Birrell and

13

Williamson 1983; Connolly 1985; Casper 1985). By contrast, the possibility of variations within Britain seems to have been largely overlooked, perhaps not least because the administrative and structural environments for community care are apparently more similar. A second limitation to our study is that the voluntary and private sectors have been given less weight than ideally they might merit. The differences in policy towards both sectors are such that they deserve independent study as is suggested, for example, in the variations in the central departments' approaches to the 'opportunities for volunteering' programme (Doyle and others 1985; Bryant 1985; the Unemployed Voluntary Action Fund 1986), and to 'contracting out' the 'hotel' services in the NHS. Our treatment of the social security system has been similarly restricted, even though the importance of interrelating policies for social security and community care is being increasingly emphasised (House of Commons Social Services Committee 1985; 1986; Working Group on Joint Planning 1985, paragraph 16.9; DHSS 1985b). However, because the DHSS has sole responsibility for administering the social security system uniformly across Britain it is not subject to the same variations which apply to those services which have been devolved to Edinburgh and Cardiff.

Community care is an appropriate vehicle for exploring variations in policy processes and outputs within Britain for two main reasons. First, as a central thrust of national policy for more than a quarter of a century it offers a useful test of the degree to which the DHSS actually operates as the lead department in policy-making for the health and personal social services. Second, the substance, no less than the long-established nature, of this policy has significance for its value as an intra-UK (or Britain) comparator.

The implementation of the community care policy is dependent upon the fulfilment of at least two fundamental conditions:

1 a shift in the balance of responsibilities and resources from the National Health Service to local authorities and voluntary organisations; and

2 an increase in inter-service coordination at all levels in policy and service delivery processes.

Both of these conditions require the establishment of more corporate approaches at the centre as well as at local level. It might be hypothesised that such an approach could more readily emerge in Scotland or Wales where a single department with a single political head has responsibility for both the substantive and financial elements of policy (an added advantage being that the health services in both countries are more generously endowed in resources than England: see Chapter 4, Table 1). By contrast, such responsibilities are not only spread across several Whitehall departments but there are also substantial differences in the scale of the governmental machine. Kellas and Madgwick (1982, page 10) offer some support for such a view, arguing that 'the territorial offices are more corporate in their organisation and style than the giant functional departments based in London'. To the extent that this observation is valid, the consequence ought to be not only more coherence in policy at the centre than is possible in England but also more coherence in central-local relationships. In other words, the policy 'message' from the centre to the various service delivery agencies with which it deals might be expected to demonstrate a greater degree of consistency than in England. A case study of community care enables us to explore such hypotheses and, in particular, the extent to which differing degrees of integration in the Scottish and Welsh Offices, respectively, facilitate shifts in responsibilities and resources between government functions compared with the more fragmented structures in England at the Whitehall level.

Finally, community care policies are appropriate for the purpose of comparative research. As Klein (1983b page 24) points out, it is necessary to be clear about the objective of an exercise in comparative research: 'the research strategy should be to concentrate on specific issues, rather than to attempt to make a general comparison of organisations and structure'. One approach to comparative research within Britain, and the one adopted here, is to take an issue – like community care – and use it as a tracer through the policy system in order to examine the process whereby inputs are translated into outputs. Blaxter (1976) adopted a similar approach in her investigation of the needs of the disabled. The case study is well suited to this tracer approach. Moreover, as Rodgers and others (1979) have argued, comparative research is best served by case studies which are defined as 'constructive descriptions'. This is because 'the case study forces one to think very hard about the context within which any social policy is developed and implemented' (page 4). We believe the context to be crucial in accounting in large measure for the varied response to the community care initiative within each of the three countries comprising Britain.

It will already be evident that our interests are not confined to the level of government departments. We have previously referred to the possibility of variations in the nature of central-local relationships in Britain. However, it is important to appreciate that community care implies the need to develop substantial degrees of inter-service coordination at three levels in the policy system:

15

the national or inter-departmental level;
the local or inter-agency level;
the field or inter-professional level.

The focus of this study is, however, upon only the first two of these levels. While each of us is currently engaged in research into multidisciplinary collaboration between fieldworkers (Cotmore and others 1985; Hunter and Cantley 1984; McKeganey and Hunter 1986; Wistow and Wray 1986), the purpose of this study is to explore variations in the policy, financial and organisational environments of such inter-professional working. Underlying our approach is the belief that variations in policy and administration are not only less well-known than they ought to be but that policy learning might result from improved knowledge of them.

PLAN OF THE BOOK

Chapters 2 to 5 concentrate on community care at central government level. Chapter 2 provides an organisational and managerial context for the subsequent analysis by reviewing the central departments in England, Scotland and Wales and, in particular, their responsibilities and management styles. We also make reference in this chapter to the nature of two sets of important relationships: centre-centre and central-local relations in each of the three countries. Chapter 3 reviews financial arrangements which may promote inter-service coordination and particularly describes the block grant system in Scotland and Wales with its inbuilt degree of flexibility to allow switches between heads of expenditure. In Chapter 4 we review the policy and planning context in each of the three countries and describe how community care has taken shape in each of them. A service and resource profile shows the differing balances between community and other services evident in England, Scotland and Wales. We then present, in Chapter 5, a case study of services for mentally handicapped people to illustrate how a key component of the community care strategy has taken very different forms in each of the three countries.

Chapters 6 and 7 concentrate on community care and inter-service coordination at the local level with particular reference to variations in the framework and mechanisms deployed by the three central departments to promote community care. In Chapter 6 we review the attempts to promote links between health and local authorities and comment on how several restructurings of the NHS over the past decade or so have affected these attempts. The various types of collaborative machinery are described across Britain and their achievements are assessed. In Chapter 7 the financial incentives for cooperation are reviewed. Significant differences in the origins, timing and content of the mechanisms are shown to exist in each of the three countries.

The conclusion, Chapter 8, links the central and local arenas that have been the subject of the preceding chapters and reviews the implications of our analysis for the salience of the concepts of the lead department, policy uniformity, administrative creativity, and policy coherence as they apply to the management of health and social care in Britain. We end with a comment on the implications of our findings for policy learning.

Chapter 2
MAPPING THE ORGANISATIONAL CONTEXT
1 CENTRAL DEPARTMENTS, BOUNDARIES
AND RESPONSIBILITIES FOR COMMUNITY CARE

INTRODUCTION

Policies for community care in Britain have varied in their emphasis and degree of specificity over the last 25 years, as we make clear in Chapter 4. At their root, however, have been two basic themes: that policies should be directed at meeting individual needs rather than producing services (for example, Ministry of Health 1963); and that this objective can best be met by replacing inherited service systems dominated by large institutions (especially long-stay hospitals) with a more balanced and flexible range of alternative services. A recent statement by the DHSS (1985a, paragraph 3, page 1) captures the essence of the policy well: 'community care is a matter of marshalling resources, sharing responsibilities and combining skills to achieve good quality modern services to meet the actual needs of real people, in ways those people find acceptable and in places which encourage rather than prevent normal living'.

The principal targets of these policies have been 'dependency groups' such as elderly, mentally handicapped and mentally ill people and it has increasingly been appreciated that an extensive range of government functions has a role in meeting their needs including health services, social services, housing, education, social security, transport, employment and physical planning. Voluntary organisations, the private sector and the informal caring networks of family and neighbourhood have also been given increasingly prominent positions in the provision of community care.

We cannot devote to each of these functions and groups of service providers the degree of attention which they might ideally merit. Consequently, we have concentrated upon the three central government functions – health, personal social services and housing – at the core of programmes for community care. In the following sections we review the distribution of community care related functions in London, Edinburgh and Cardiff together with the arrangements for their administration by the central departments in each of the three countries.

18

and the SDG was increased, with officials from the former 'shadowing' each policy division or branch. The aim of this approach was, in part, to ensure that cost containment and cost effectiveness considerations figured more prominently in the policy development process.

Policy coherence within the DHSS

A number of formal mechansims have been established within the Department with the objective of achieving policy coordination across service boundaries. The client group teams have this purpose at one level. At another, the Health and Personal Social Services Strategy Committee, chaired by the first Permanent Secretary, is designed to bring together the work of the various administrative groups on the major policy issues affecting these services. A smiliar strategy committee exists for social security matters. The principal formal mechanism spanning the various wings of the Department has been the Cross-Sector Policy Review Group, chaired by the head of the Social Services Inspectorate. However, some officials sense that less emphasis may have been accorded to it in the period immediately following the implementation of the Griffiths report (DHSS 1983c) on health services management (see below). At the same time the role at the 'top of the office' of the Departmental Management Board may be assuming more prominence. The Board is chaired by the first permanent secretary and made up of the three officials of second permanent secretary rank (Social Security, Chairman of the NHS Management Board, and Chief Medical Officer) together with the Principal Finance and Principal Establishments Officers.

Despite the existence of such mechanisms for inter-sectoral coordination, the Department's capacity to achieve a coherent approach to policies for health, personal social services and social security has been strongly questioned in recent years. The House of Commons Social Services Committee was especially critical on this point recording:

> ... its disappointment – and dismay – at the continuing failure of the DHSS to adopt a coherent policy strategy across the administrative boundaries of individual services and programmes ... We recommend that the DHSS should give high priority to developing its capacity for devising coherent policy strategies for all the areas for which the Secretary of State is responsible. (House of Commons Social Services Committee 1980, paragraph 15, page viii)

Partly in response to such criticisms, a Policy Strategy Unit was established within the DHSS to carry out, *inter alia*, policy reviews across the whole range of the Department's responsibilities. However, prior to its recent demise its work had assumed a lower profile and the

23

Unit's former head, a career civil servant, has suggested that its coordinating role – as provider of the secretariat to the major internal policy committees – had 'proved the most durable element, and that its policy analyses have had only limited impact' (James 1983, page 60).

More generally, it is probably true to say that the interaction between, and substitutability of, services and social security benefits have not, in the past, been prominent items on the public agenda of the Department. This view is borne out not only by Nairne's comment on the absence of trade-offs quoted earlier but also by the rapid expansion in recent years of private residential and nursing homes, especially for the elderly. Fuelled very largely by social security payments, Klein (1985, page 203) has argued: 'there is no evidence that this represents a deliberate or explicit policy decision, as distinct from an accidental side-effect of social security programmes framed with totally different purposes in mind'. Whatever the case, it is certainly difficult to reconcile vastly increased access to institutional care in the private sector, based on financial criteria rather than levels of dependency, with DHSS objectives for the public sector which emphasise care in the community and the more rigorous targeting of services on identified needs. Concern about this and a number of other policy contradictions and unintended consequences (Wistow 1986) have thrust this issue high on the public policy agenda. The Department, in conjunction with the local authority associations, produced a report on this subject in 1985 (DHSS 1985b). A number of policy options designed to resolve these difficulties is currently being studied by a further joint working party. Within the Department the issue is under intensive review by, among other vehicles, the Cross-Sector Policy Review Group. Already, as a step towards bringing the two sides of the Department closer together, senior officials have been moved from PSS to social security and vice versa (House of Commons Social Services Committee 1986, volume 1, paragraph 81).

Nonetheless, on the available evidence, there are grounds for some scepticism about the extent of coordination between the two main wings of the DHSS, certainly up until very recently. In its wide-ranging examination of community care the House of Commons Social Services Committee noted that 'a considerable number of social security problems arise from community care policies' and recorded its 'impression that they have not always been fully appreciated by those responsible for social security policy formation' (House of Commons Social Services Committee 1985, paragraph 146, page xxv). The Department firmly rebutted this charge in its response to the Committee's report: 'community care and social security policies have not been developed without regard for each other' (DHSS 1985b, paragraph 35, page 10). However, when subsequently questioned by the Committee about the Department's ability to measure the effect of community care policies on both sides of its budget the former Minister of Social Security conceded 'We are not as good as we would like to be; we are conscious of that' (House of Commons Social Services Committee 1986, volume 1, paragraph 81). It is clear that social security benefits are playing a more substantial role in community care and that increased collaboration between income support and care services is necessary not only at national level but also at local level, a point recognised in the report of a working group on joint planning jointly established by the DHSS and the health and local authority associations (Working Group on Joint Planning 1985, paragraph 16.9, page 33). The rapid growth of social security payments in support of private residential care further underlines this point.

FINANCE DRIVEN
FOLLOW the £

Implementation of the Griffiths report

The inquiry into NHS management, led by Roy Griffiths, deputy chairman and managing director of the Sainsbury's supermarket group, was critical of the lack of coherence in the DHSS's relationship with the health service (DHSS 1983c). The implementation of the inquiry team's recommendations has led to changes in the internal structure of the DHSS which are of recent origin (House of Commons Social Services Committee 1985, page 91) and whose consequences cannot, therefore, be fully determined.

The changes, which in the view of the former permanent secretary, Sir Patrick Nairne, reflect 'a shift from structural organisation to managerial reform' (Nairne 1983, page 243), follow very largely from Griffiths' criticism that none of the DHSS groups and officials was 'concerned full-time with the totality of NHS management' and that a clearly defined general management function was missing at all levels in the service. Outside the Department, the consensus-based multi-disciplinary management teams have been replaced by the appointment of general managers at regional, district and unit levels. Within it, an NHS Supervisory Board and a Management Board have been established, as Griffiths recommended, to provide an internal general management capacity. The membership of these boards is shown in Figure 1.

The Supervisory Board is chaired by the Secretary of State while the Management Board was led by Victor Paige, a businessman appointed on a three-year contract in January 1985 as the full-time 'general manager of the NHS'. Paige resigned in 1986, only halfway through his contract, stating that he was unhappy with the political and

Figure 1   Divisional structure of DHSS HQ[1]

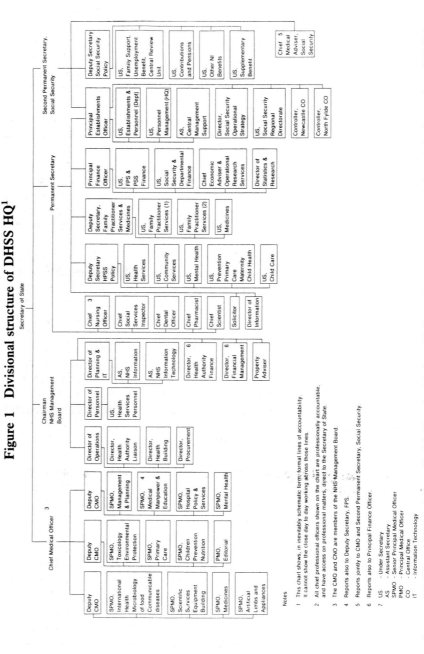

Notes

1 This chart shows, in inevitably schematic form, formal lines of accountability. It cannot show the close day to day working across those lines.

2 All chief professional officers shown on the chart are professionally accountable, and have access on professional matters, direct to the Secretary of State.

3 The CMO and CNO are members of the NHS Management Board

4 Reports also to Deputy Secretary, FPS

5 Reports jointly to CMO and Second Permanent Secretary, Social Security.

6 Reports also to Principal Finance Officer.

7 US   - Under Secretary
   AS   - Assistant Secretary
   SPMO - Senior Principal Medical Officer
   PMO   - Principal Medical Officer
   CO   - Central Office
   IT   - Information Technology

Source: DHSS and Welsh Office, Health Trends, 18, 2, p 36. Reproduced with the permission of the Controller of HMSO.

bureaucratic constraints on management at the centre: 'Ministers and the Chairman of the Management Board can approach the same issues with different priorities, objectives and restraints. Also there are always others in the action – or trying to be'. While holding the rank of second permanent secretary in the Department, Paige's salary of £75,000 was then considerably in excess of normal civil service scales for that rank of official. The NHS Management Board includes a Director of Health Authority Liaison and its first holder had previously headed regional liaison within the RG. His successor believes that the main role of the regional liaison division is a 'primary line of communication' with health authorities – it provides a 'readily available contact point for those wanting some explanation of government policy' (Davies 1986b). Regional liaison is at the 'sharp edge' of relations between the centre and the periphery and endeavours to steer a steady course between letting general managers manage on the one hand and holding them to account on the other.

Also uncertain are the implications of Griffiths for inter-service coordination, particularly with the personal social services. Hitherto, much DHSS policy for the personal social services has been inseparable from that for the health service. Collaboration has been considered fundamental, in particular, to the implementation of priority group and community care policies. Yet neither the Social Services Inspectorate nor the SDG (now renamed the Policy Group) are directly represented on the Supervisory or Management Boards. Relations between health and social services were identified as one of the six initial areas of priority for the Supervisory Board (Stowe 1984) but DHSS membership of a working group which recently reviewed joint planning and joint finance included no officials from the NHS Management Board (Working Group on Joint Planning 1985).

Perhaps too much should not be read into the composition of such formal structures. Most recently, the Permanent Secretary at the DHSS told the House of Commons Social Services Committee that care in the community was to top the agenda at the next meeting between the NHS Management Board and regional health authority chairmen (House of Commons Social Services Committee 1986, volume 2, page 127). Moreover, the Management Board has been devoting considerable attention to the production of a national corporate plan for the NHS (Halpern 1986a). It remains to be seen, however, how far the emphasis on strengthening management and accountability arrangements within the health service will affect the influence of the policy branches and their boundary spanning client group planning remits.

ADMINISTRATIVE ARRANGEMENTS FOR SCOTLAND

The Acts of Union of 1707 merged the parliaments of Scotland and England but there was no equivalent merger at the administrative level. Although the Scottish Office and post of Secretary of State were not created until 1885, Scotland was managed by Scots and Scottish departments through a system of decentralised administration (Kellas 1980). From its creation in 1885 until the present day, the Scottish Office has grown both in size and in the extent of its functions. Nevertheless, cuts in civil service manpower have reduced the number of officials by one-fifth since 1976 leaving a total of under 9000 civil servants. This has inevitably caused strains when the range of functions has not shown similar signs of diminishing (Gibson 1985b). An important difference to bear in mind between Edinburgh and London is the predominance of professional advisers in the Scottish Office. From the middle to the upper reaches of the Office they outnumber the administrators by two to one.

Most of the functions initially assumed by the Scottish Office were transferred from the Home Office although the latter was reluctant to lose its hold over Scotland. After a few years the Scottish Office became accepted as the agency of central government for purely Scottish affairs and the Scottish Secretary was regarded as 'Scotland's Minister'. Before 1939 the Scottish Office operated from Dover House, its London base which still exists, with only a small outpost in Edinburgh. The Gilmour report on Scottish administration published in 1937 paved the way for the shift of activities from London to Edinburgh.

Despite its separatism and growth, the Scottish Office has arguably not completely shed its Home Office origins. For example, a longstanding observer of the Scottish Office asserts that the Scottish Office suffers from a basic 'lack of curiosity' (Hanham 1985) for which he suggests that the legacy of the Home Office may be largely responsible. It is, after all, not a department renowned for a far-sighted innovative approach to policy. Of all the Whitehall departments the Home Office is the most defensive, secretive and resistant to change, reflecting the somewhat negative character of many of its responsibilities which centre upon law and order (Bonham-Carter 1981). According to Hanham the Scottish Office is imbued with a similar ethos.

Elsewhere, Hanham (1969, page 68) has written that Scottish administration has 'retained a slightly old-fashioned bureaucratic flavour'. Hood and Dunsire (1981, page 215) in a study of central departments and their differences, interpret this to mean one or more of four attributes: '(a) a greater use of formal regulation than in the general run of departments; (b) a reluctance to publish policy statements, and relatively little direct or face-to-face communication with the public; (c) a "quill-pen" type of office procedure; and (d) a disinclination to pursue research'. Hood and Dunsire did not find evidence to substantiate any of these attributes with the possible exception of a tendency for Scottish Office departments to show signs of a 'regulation-heavy' style. Indeed, Hood and Dunsire conclude that the whole is more than the sum of the parts and that it is only when a large number of dimensions are studied that the distinctiveness of Scottish administration (and probably Welsh administration for that matter) becomes apparent. Looked at in this way, the authors claim that, taken as a group, 'the Scottish Office departments are significantly different from the Whitehall group on several matters of structure and style of operation' including high functional complexity, the relatively high senior staff component of departments, and a larger number of fringe bodies (page 230).

Internal organisation of the Scottish Office★

Since 1973 the Scottish Office has comprised five departments, three of which share an involvement in community care policy – the Scottish Home and Health Department (SHHD), the Scottish Education Department (SED), and the Scottish Development Department (SDD), and a group of central services divisions. The Secretary of State for Scotland is a Minister of Cabinet rank. Currently aided by a ministerial team of four, he covers the policy fields of at least six English Secretaries of State, albeit for a tenth of the population (5.2 million).

Each department is under the charge of a Secretary who is responsible to the Secretary of State for the work of his department. The Permanent Under Secretary of State is general adviser to the Secretary of State and directly supervises the work of the central services divisions. Under the chairmanship of the Permanent Under Secretary of State the heads of departments constitute a Management Group to ensure coordination of work, to consider common problems across the whole field of Scottish Office responsibilities, and to advise the Secretary of State and his ministerial team. Junior ministers in the Scottish Office generally enjoy a greater degree of autonomy than is accorded to their English counterparts as well as a higher profile (Davies 1986a).

★ The Scottish Office was unable to provide an organisation chart equivalent to those for England and Wales and reproduced in Figures 1 and 2.

While appearances may suggest that by bringing together a range of functions under a single Minister, the Scottish Office is able to take a more corporate view of policy and administration and to achieve a greater degree of coordination than is possible in England, it would be wrong to view the Scottish Office as monolithic in its operation. Functions are divided between its departments, often in a curious way as, for example, in the case of health and social work services (see below). In common with other Whitehall departments, fragmentation and departmentalism have been persistent managerial and structural problems within the Scottish Office and its five departments. Indeed, they can on occasion be even more acute. 'The old, intense departmental loyalties', as Gibson (1985b, page 164) puts it, remain much in evidence. Civil servants see the need for a Scottish Office *esprit de corps* but 'the fierce loyalties felt for the individual departments . . . have not yet been fully replaced by a strong Scottish Office loyalty' (page 181). As Keating and Midwinter (1983, page 16) report, 'specialist interests maintained substantive policy autonomy in functional departments. The result was a largely 'symbolic', reactive role for the Secretary of State, rather than priority determination'. But there are countervailing pressures. In particular, Ministers and officials are required to be generalists rather than specialists. Because there are fewer civil servants in the Scottish Office than their Whitehall counterparts (but more than in Wales) they range over a wider area in their work. One individual's scope of responsibility will generally correspond to that of around six counterparts in Whitehall (Gibson 1985b).* Gibson suggests that this 'width of view' can be a help in Whitehall bargaining.

The SHHD, with a staff complement of about 850, is responsible for the NHS in Scotland. Most of the Department's budget is allocated to the NHS. The NHS is administered by 15 health boards which are, with one exception, coterminous with the regional (or islands') authorities responsible for social work services and education (and housing in the islands' councils). The exception is the four boards which fall within the boundaries of Strathclyde Region which is Scotland's largest local authority (and Britain's after the demise of the Greater London Council and the Metropolitan counties). The boards are responsible for family practitioner services, unlike the position in England after 1985. Housing is a district council function except in the islands. The SHHD performs some of the functions of a regional

---

* Writing in 1975, Kellas calculated that one civil servant in Edinburgh covered the ground of three in Whitehall with only one-tenth of the clientele. Gibson's more recent figures may reflect the reduction in manpower levels coupled with an increasing workload.

health authority in England in addition to the traditional civil service functions carried out by central departments in Whitehall. There is, therefore, a different type of central-local relationship in Scotland (as there is in Wales) with the central department more directly involved in a managerial capacity at the operational level in specific matters. To aid the Department in these functions a number of departmental and quasi-autonomous agencies operate at national level. The arrangements were introduced following the first major reorganisation of the NHS in 1974 and have not been greatly disturbed by subsequent changes.

A multi-professional planning unit located within the SHHD is charged with the review and development of planning for the NHS. Its staff are drawn from the civil service. The planning council, positioned between the SHHD and the health boards, is a source of advice to the Secretary of State and acts as a bridging mechanism between the government and the health service in Scotland. Since 1985 the Secretary of the Planning Council has divided his time between the Council and the Unit. A number of national consultative committees exist for each of the main health service professions and provide a source of specialist advice to the Planning Council. The work of the Council is considered in more detail in Chapter 4 in the section on health priorities and planning.

The Common Services Agency (CSA) provides a range of all-Scotland services (for example, information, supplies, blood transfusion) under joint NHS/SHHD management. Management responsiblity rests with a management committee appointed by the Secretary of State, six of whose members are jointly nominated by health boards. Its composition reflects national and local interests and is intended to be a partnership between the SHHD and health boards. The CSA is not a compact, monolithic organisation but a loose federation of agencies each providing a different service. The existence of the CSA is testimony to the trend in recent years noted by Gibson (1985b), namely, the deliberate, if not always successful, withdrawal by the Scottish Office from involvement in the day-to-day running of services.

Public education is supervised by the SED acting in cooperation with the local authorities which are directly responsible for the service within their areas. The Department generally supervises provision for community education, including youth, community and adult education, and it gives grants to a number of voluntary organisations. It looks after the Secretary of State's responsibilities for the arts and for sport and physical recreation. There is no readily observable link between the activities of the SED and those belonging to the SHHD which relate to the educational dimension of the priority care groups.

The SED is also responsible for social work which is organised separately from the main Department and enjoys little direct contact with it. The Social Work Services Group (SWSG) has been attached to the Department since 1968 when social work was reorganised in Scotland. The Minister covering the SED is not responsible for the SWSG (see below). Until recently, administrators have been organised in four divisions, and 30 professional advisers, who collectively formed the Central Advisory Service (CAS), have been organised into nine teams. Following an internal scrutiny of the CAS, administrative and professional staff comprising the SWSG have been integrated into four new divisions (Moyes 1985).

The efficiency scrutiny of CAS was highly critical of the Advisory Service's activities and among the report's 17 recommendations were that the SWSG should give greater emphasis to policy analysis and development, and to the dissemination of good practice. The report also suggested that the possibility of locating the SWSG within the SHHD should be studied with a view to eliminating overlap in the work of the two departments (see below).

Although there exists no obvious reason why the SWSG is located within the SED there are a number of pointers which combine service considerations with administrative ones. In 1960 child care functions were transferred from the former Scottish Home Department to the SED foreshadowing, and perhaps giving a lead to, later developments in social work. Departmental size proved to be a factor of some importance. According to a senior official:

> ...there had to be a balancing act...trying to get departments of more or less equal size, and we came to be associated with the smallest department at that time.

Finally, in the trilogy of departments with an input into community care policy is the SDD which is, *inter alia*, responsible for housing, general policy on local government, and transport. The Department was established in 1962 and took over many of the responsibilities of the former Scottish Home Department, such as local government, and of the Department of Health for Scotland, such as housing. The links between the SHHD and the SDD with regard to health care and housing policy appear less integrated and well developed than is formally the position between the SHHD and the SWSG. Although there is fairly regular informal contact between housing and social work there is no formal input into service planning. Currently the Housing Division is urging local authorities to concentrate their new build activities on the provision of special needs housing and to adapt existing stock for use by the elderly and by the mentally and physically handicapped. It is hoped that more widespread availability of sheltered housing for the elderly and initiatives such as the Key Housing Association homes for the mentally handicapped will reduce pressure on NHS bed space. The most recent SDD statistics show that the number of all public sector 'special needs housing' has increased from 12,600 in 1979 to 37,000 in 1985 (personal communication). Special needs housing is also sponsored or provided by the Housing Corporation and the Scottish Special Housing Association.

In relation to transport, the SDD is responsible for policy in respect of the Scottish Transport Group, a nationalised industry providing bus services and the main west coast shipping services to the islands. As with education, transport considerations do not figure prominently in policy development for the priority care groups.

Policy coherence within the Scottish Office

Since 1979 there has been a Minister for Health and Social Work embracing the functions of the SHHD and the SWSG. (Between 1985 and 1986 Home Affairs were included in the ministerial brief; following the September 1986 ministerial reshuffle, the Highlands and Islands and Tourism have been substituted.) Officials maintain that the joint health and social work brief was a recognition of 'the natural links that have been forged...with SHHD' and of 'the natural association of the work, the common purpose'. It is difficult to gauge the impact of this political change on policy and practice. Generally it is seen as beneficial although integration has been slow. As one official expressed it, 'there has been a steady progress towards at least making sure that we consult our opposite numbers and more recently a greater integration of policy-making'. A number of examples are cited as evidence of this closer working relationship, including the circular on community care, joint planning and support finance (Scottish Office 1985), and the interdepartmental working group which is revising health priorities in Scotland (see Chapter 4). Nevertheless, it is perhaps significant to note that, in contrast to the practice elsewhere in Britain, in Scotland only the Minister for Health and Social Work has responsibilities which cut across the two departments. At the official level only the most senior civil servant in the Scottish Office – the Permanent Under Secretary of State – exercises similar responsibilities.

Not surprisingly, in view of their differing traditions and distinct organisational separation, there is not complete harmonisation. Moreover, the two departments, SHHD and SED (SWSG), relate to the periphery in quite different ways which in large part reflects the different financing and organisation of health boards and local authorities.

33

These factors shape the respective operating styles of the SHHD and the SWSG. Whereas the SHHD is more directive in its relationship with health boards (although this is not in evidence on all occasions, thereby emphasising the ambivalence of the Scottish Office which attempts to operate a 'hands off' policy and to provide strategic direction to activities within its control), the SWSG's stance is essentially advisory and persuasive since local authorities cannot be cajoled and ultimately must be left to determine their own priorities.

In a study of collaboration between the SHHD and the SWSG (and their respective relations with the field) prior to the introduction of a joint ministerial post, Wiseman (1979) found that officials experienced difficulty in handling conflicts and in working across administrative boundaries. He offered a number of reasons for this. First, the departmental structure of the Scottish Office required that one department take the 'lead' (in health policy this meant the SHHD); second, the 'lead' department was more likely to consult with others rather than participate jointly in exploring issues in which there was an obvious conflict (the health priorities document produced in 1980 appears to have been the product of such a culture); third, ministers were usually not consulted in the early stages of policy development; fourth, the multiple goals and objectives pursued by the SHHD and the SWSG made joint working difficult and potential conflict more likely; finally, a reluctance to challenge received wisdom or previously agreed policy positions (for example, the SHHD's policy of not earmarking funds to health boards, and the reluctance of the SWSG to issue guidance to local authorities which could be construed as having financial implications) made it more difficult for the two sides to find common ground.

It is unlikely that a great deal has changed since Wiseman reached these conclusions, and the efficiency scrutiny of the CAS mentioned above lends support to this view. Moyes (1985, paragraph 87, page 25) reported that many in the social work field regarded 'the improvement of liaison between social work departments and the NHS [as] one of the major issues currently facing social work'. The transfer of the SWSG would be an important step towards achieving this. The report said there was a strong case for locating the SWSG and the SHHD in the same building. 'The present physical distance between the two clearly prevents the casual contact which is so often what good liaison boils down to' (paragraph 90, page 26). Another suggestion for bringing the two departments closer together was for the Scottish Office to establish client group teams along the lines of those in the DHSS.

Despite the continuing search for a means of resolving coordination problems, the existence of a Minister for Health and Social Work may

34

have had some effect on relations between the two camps. If nothing else there is probably symbolic value attached to the post which provides an opportunity for an integrated approach even if it remains to be fully realised. However, while a possible antidote to narrow departmentalism, in such circumstances it becomes possible for officials, perhaps for the best of motives, to restrict the range of issues brought to Ministers' attention.

Of course the issue of interdepartmental working is much more than a structural matter. Individuals, their personalities and operating styles, are of crucial importance in any interaction. Nevertheless departmental tradition and culture can either aid or impede interpersonal contact and contribute to frontier problems. Wiseman's point about an absence of direct political input at the formative stages of policy development while not peculiar to the Scottish Office is particularly acute there and remains pertinent. It is a fact of political life that Ministers are frequently absent on business in London leaving officials some 400 miles away in charge for much of the time of what has been termed the 'concrete Kremlin' (Gibson 1985a). Writing about the management of Scottish education, Mackintosh (1976, page 113) argues that:

> ... it is hard to say who takes the decisions or provides the leadership. One thing is clear. The Scottish politicians can contribute little. They have, perhaps, one 2½-hour debate a year on the subject plus some questions. Cooped up in Westminster during the week and running from one constituency engagement to the next at weekends, they cannot be in touch with all the aspects of the educational scene at home.

The health service is no different. The centre of the political stage is in Westminster and not in Edinburgh. The significance of this geopolitical factor should not be lightly dismissed; it does not apply to Wales to quite the same degree where shorter distances between the two centres of government reduce the need for prolonged absences. Compounding the issue of political control, or its absence, is the tradition in Scotland, as previously noted, of ministerial responsibilities spanning a number of departments and policy fields not all of which may seem obviously related.

Implementation of the Griffiths report

With the advent of the Griffiths report on NHS management there have been some modest changes in the organisation of the central health department in Scotland. As elsewhere in Britain, the NHS in Scotland has its general manager within the SHHD although, unlike elsewhere, he is a career civil servant of under secretary rank. Within the Department a Policy Board has been established chaired by the Minister for Health and Social Work. Its membership is as follows:

SHHD Policy Board membership
Minister for Health and Social Work (Chairman);
Senior officials of SHHD – CMO, CNO, Secretary;
Chairman of Scottish Health Service Planning Council;
Chairman of Health Board Chairmen's Group;
Chief Scientist;
2 private sector appointments.

In order to service the new arrangements the Department has rearranged itself into two groups responsible for policy and management respectively. Each is headed by an under secretary with the nominal head of the NHS in Scotland responsible for the Management Group. This post brings together a group of reorganised divisions concerned with NHS management, operational planning, finance and performance monitoring. The policy planning activities of the Policy Group include primary health care and longer term health policy which involves liaising with the Planning Council. They come within the second under secretary's responsibilities, as do personnel and Whitley Council matters. Unlike England, where management and policy matters have been split between someone appointed from outside the civil service (as in Wales) and the permanent secretary of the DHSS respectively, in Scotland the responsibilities have been split between two internal civil servants, one of whom was new to health.

Many of the ideas contained in the Griffiths report are not new to Scotland where the arguments in favour of chief executives (or general managers) for the NHS were originally aired some 20 years ago in the (Farquharson-Lang) report of an official committee set up to make recommendations on the improvement of the administrative practice of hospital boards (SHHD 1966). Much of the managerial philosophy and quest for greater efficiency and effectiveness which emerged forcefully as central themes in Griffiths' proposals can be found in that report.

Griffiths echoed Farquharson-Lang in favouring a single channel of management and administration to improve policy coherence and accountability. Just as the Griffiths report said much that was true of Scotland, Farquharson-Lang said much that applied to England and Wales. But in the mid 1960s the proposal for general managers was quietly set aside. Such an approach went against the growing tide in favour of multidisciplinary team management based on consensus.

Events in Scotland with regard to Griffiths' application to the NHS have generally followed those in England although there are ministerial claims that the issue of general management was already on the agenda in Scotland in advance of Griffiths (Davies 1986a). Whatever the sequence of events, differences in style and in timing and pace of activity can be detected (Hunter 1984). Perhaps most important, the evident zeal for Griffiths in England displayed by the Secretary of State for Social Services and the then Minister for Health was absent in Scotland. A possible explanation is that the Griffiths proposals fitted a coherent strategy to improve management that was already unfolding in England (for example, annual performance reviews, performance indicators, efficiency savings, contracting out). Developments in Scotland have been less obviously coherent or ideologically based but rather more pragmatic and reactive in character. For example, the introduction of general management at unit level in late 1986, some considerable time after England, followed a report commissioned by the SHHD from a firm of management consultants, Coopers and Lybrand Associates (SHHD 1986a). At the same time, in the accompanying SHHD circular on the development of senior management structures, there is a heavy emphasis on the need for a corporate approach which has certainly been less apparent in England (SHHD 1986b). In this respect, developments in Scotland are closer to those in Wales. The Scottish circular says that 'a range of professional skills must be brought together in pursuit of the [Health] Board's objectives, plans and programmes to provide a comprehensive service within its area' (SHHD 1986b, paragraph 8, page 2). This calls for the participation in the management effort of a senior nurse, a senior doctor and a senior finance officer. Similar arrangements are to prevail at unit level. It appears, then, that the concept of consensus or team management remains alive in Scotland, particularly when it is appreciated that the senior nursing and medical officers in the management team will not simply advise the general manager but will also have a separate right of access to the Board on matters arising from their professional responsibilities and involving the exercise of their professional judgement. The position in England is much less clear cut.

Having waited upon events in England before acting, what has emerged (and is still emerging) in Scotland is the product of a blend of influences rather than a direct transfer of English practice as the two official pronouncements on the subject make clear (SHHD 1984; 1985).

ADMINISTRATIVE ARRANGEMENTS FOR WALES

Responsibility for economic and social policy matters within Wales is vested in the Welsh Office and its political head, the Secretary of State for Wales, a post first established as recently as 1964. In social policy matters it is also a 'young' department; responsibility for health and PSS was transferred from the DHSS only in 1969 and 1971 respectively. They come together in the Health and Social Work Department. The health service in Wales is administered through nine district health authorities (DHAs) and eight family practitioner committees. Seven DHAs enjoy one-to-one coterminosity with the county councils, the level of local government which is responsible for providing personal social services. In Dyfed, however, two health authorities were established within the county's boundaries as part of the 1982 restructuring of the health service.

In formal terms, the division of responsibilities is as follows: with the exception of health, all the main services providing community care are administered by local government, that is, personal social services, housing and education. The major differences between Wales on the one hand, and England and Scotland on the other hand are in the scale of the administrative machine (reflecting the size of the Welsh population which, at 2.8 million, is roughly half that of Scotland and smaller than that of all but four English RHAs) and in the degree of administrative integration which this permits within the Welsh Office itself.

Internal organisation of the Welsh Office

A single deputy secretary covers all the major social policy functions, including education. However, education is administered as a separate division and is combined with the predominatly economic policy responsibilities of one of the department's two junior ministers. The administrative and political integration of housing, health and social service functions is closer (see Figure 2). All of these – together with responsibility for local government – are included within the remit of the second junior minister. The responsibilities of individual civil servants are similarly extensive. Thus, housing, health and social services policy matters have, since 1985, been the responsibility of an under secretary, the level at which, for example, responsibility for all child care and all mental health matters is located within the DHSS. An indication of the scale of the administrative machine in Wales is that the Health Policy Division has only 167 staff, about half of which are clerical. Generally speaking, the ratio of Welsh Office civil servants to their counterparts in Whitehall Departments is about one to ten. (As noted earlier, in the Scottish Office one estimate puts it at one to six.)

Like the SHHD, the Welsh Office has a dual function in relation to the health service. It exercises both a traditional civil service function and also carries out some aspects of the regional role in health matters.

Figure 2 Welsh Office – housing, health and social services functions

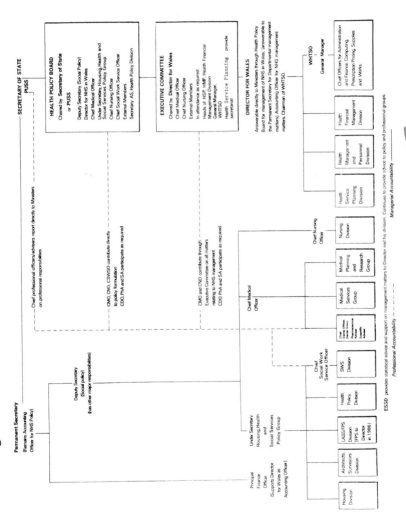

Source: Welsh Office Circular WHC(85)24, 1985.

Central services such as supplies, major building projects and so on are provided through the Welsh Health Common Services Authority, formerly called the Welsh Health Technical Services Organisation (WHTSO), which is similar in function to the Scottish CSA. The WHTSO was set up at the same time as the Scottish CSA in 1974. WHTSO was managed by a special health authority comprised of a chairman appointed by the Secretary of State, three members appointed by the Secretary of State, three members nominated by the health authorities, and two other members nominated by the Secretary of State after consultation with the health authorities. In the early days the three members appointed by the Secretary of State were officials of the Welsh Office but over the past five years or so two of the three places have gone to 'outsiders', that is, members from outside the Welsh Office and the NHS. Over the years there has been a number of quite significant differences between the Welsh Office and WHTSO. Unlike the Scottish CSA, WHTSO is not jointly managed. In August 1985, its name was changed to the Welsh Health Common Services Authority headed by a general manager. In certain respects, then, the new grouping resembles the Scottish Agency which is also headed by a general manager. There is a variety of other All Wales machinery to compensate for the absence of a regional level in health policy (see Button 1984).

Policy coherence within the Welsh Office

Structural barriers to inter-service coordination are considerably less pronounced within the Welsh Office than between Whitehall Departments or even between Scottish Office Departments, if only in the sense that issues cutting across several functions can be brought together at a relatively low level in both the political and administrative hierarchies. This advantage is reinforced by the arrangements for financing services in Wales (see Chapter 3) and in the ease of informal contacts within the Welsh Office. Officials suggested that the latter were facilitated by a number of factors, including: the small scale of the Welsh Office and the many opportunities for informal relationships afforded by relatively small numbers of staff all being accommodated within a single building; the continuity in post of senior civil servants at under secretary level and above (seven years in the case of the previous under secretary for health and social work); and specialisation between the social policy and economic policy 'wings'. While there was relatively little movement between the two wings, a considerable amount of movement by administrators at the less senior level was more frequent within them. Thus there was interchange between and within health, housing, social work and education. An administrator could, for example, work in health for a number of years and move across to special needs housing, an area where interaction with health and social services policy could be considerable.

In common with Scottish Office practice, at principal and assistant secretary levels, therefore, it was common for officials to have a much wider range of experience than in Whitehall. This was said to provide individual officials with 'an insight on the social side into the opportunities . . . for corporate planning and for having fairly rounded ways of tackling problems'. For all these reasons, systems-wide thinking across functional boundaries was said to be an established 'habit of mind' which was etched into routine patterns of working.

One instance of this – and a clear contrast with situation in both England and Scotland – was the inclusion of the Chief Social Work Service Officer in the membership of the post-Griffiths Health Policy Board. It was suggested that this was never questioned:

> . . . it is now so much part of the culture of the place that you don't take decisions about health policy without looking at the wider social implications of them. And [the Chief Social Work Service Officer] was there with the Chief Medical Officer and the Chief Nursing Officer as a matter of course.

The culture of informal team working also meant that formal structures, such as the DHSS client group teams, were now considered unnecessary although, as we reported above, they have been mooted in Scotland only recently. Client group planning teams existed in the mid 1970s but the frustrations of running them, together with the comparatively small numbers of administrative and professional staff, had helped to prompt a more selective and *ad hoc* approach to client group planning. Informal day-to-day interaction within the department was supplemented by formal working groups only when a specific task was identified. The establishment of an *ad hoc* working party to produce a strategy for services for mentally handicapped people had been the pre-eminent example of this approach. A less formal working group within the department had subsequently been considering the need for changing patterns of care for the elderly in the community.

In both cases 'lead responsibility' for coordinating policy development had fallen to social services rather than health groups within the Welsh Office. It was anticipated that this serial process of policy review would continue, with attention being directed towards mental illness once a strategy for the elderly had been accepted and mechanisms for its implementation put in place. In this case, however, it seemed likely that 'lead responsibility' would fall to the health divisions, due to the greater medical and nursing involvement in the client group.

Implementation of the Griffiths report

The implementation of the Griffiths report in Wales resulted in an internal reorganisation of the Welsh Office. The former Health and Social Work Department was divided into two parts: one a Housing, Health and Social Services Policy Group and the other a Directorate responsible for the management of the NHS (Welsh Office 1985c) (see Figure 2, page 39). This basic distinction between 'policy' on the one hand and 'management' on the other reflects the division of responsibilities between the Permanent Secretary (who remains the accounting officer for NHS policy) and the Director of the NHS in Wales who became the accounting officer for management matters. The current Director, while an outsider in terms of the NHS in Wales, is a former NHS administrator and has also had extensive experience of the private health care sector.

The top tiers of these administrative arrangements are: a Health Policy Board under the chairmanship of the Secretary of State 'to help him develop and monitor health and *social* policies for Wales' (Welsh Office 1985c, paragraph 2.1, emphasis added); and an Executive Committee of that Board, chaired by the Director of the NHS in Wales and charged with responsibility for implementing the Secretary of State's policies. The full implications of this reorganisation for inter-service coordination had yet to emerge. There was some feeling that the 'natural tendency' for the larger and directly managed health service to receive more Departmental attention might be reinforced by the establishment of the Directorate. This was potentially counterbalanced, however, by two other factors: the apparently broad health and social policy remit of the Policy Board, and the removal of management responsibility for directly managing the NHS from the Under Secretary for housing, health and social services policy, who is a member of the Board along with the Chief Social Work Service Officer. Under the previous arrangements, the Under Secretary was inevitably 'deeply engrossed' in detailed issues of health service and the role provided less space for social services policy matters than ought now to be the case. The orientation of the post may also reflect the interests and experience of individuals holding it; the present post holder, for example, had previously been responsible for housing policy rather than health service management.

One of the early public indications of the balance established between health and social services considerations will be the publication of a corporate plan for the NHS on which the Directorate was working during the summer and autumn of 1985. Although a plan for health services, it was considered 'inconceivable . . . that it would not mention the potency of joint planning and the necessity of joint planning'. At the time of writing the corporate plan had not emerged and was still being considered (Hyde 1986). Surprisingly, in view of the emphasis placed upon joint planning, the most recent (1985) priorities statement (see Chapter 4 for further details) did not give an explicit endorsement to the importance of joint planning.

The application of Griffiths' proposals to the NHS in Wales has been broadly in line with that in England. The guidance issued to health authorities, however, was much more detailed than that issued by the DHSS. Indeed, the Scottish guidance on unit management and senior management structures more closely resembles the equivalent Welsh Office circulars although, consistent with the Scottish Office's policy of disengagement, remains less detailed. In Wales, detailed job descriptions for senior officers were issued in two lengthy circulars (Welsh Office 1984a and b).

SUMMARY

It might be hypothesised that opportunities for administrative and political integration would be greater within the Scottish and Welsh Offices than in Whitehall. Our evidence so far, however, suggests that the real situation might be more complex. The structural divisions between health and personal social services at the centre appear to be greater in Scotland than in either England or Wales. The call for a client group structure in the SHHD to bring together the fragmented health and social work interests is an acknowledgement of such fragmentation and departmentalism. Nonetheless, there are also very substantial differences between the Welsh Office and Whitehall. In the Welsh Office, the blurring of administrative boundaries, the culture of informal team working, and more extensive political integration, all contribute to the creation of a substantially different context for the formulation and implementation of policies across functional boundaries. While the smaller scale is undoubtedly a key factor, it is insufficient to account fully for the differences. Were it to do so then the problems of departmentalism and fragmentation would be even greater in England than in Scotland but, on our evidence, this does not appear to be the case.

A major change in the management of the NHS in Britain merits comment, particularly since its purpose is mainly to overcome elements of the fragmentation referred to above. The Griffiths report undoubtedly has implications for community care, and therefore for our main theme, but it is too early to assess what precisely these might be. However, as we reported, the interpretation and implementation of the Griffiths proposals across the three countries has varied. The resulting differences are not insignificant but neither are they major. They are most apparent between England and Wales on the one hand and Scotland on the other (Hunter 1984). While it would appear that the DHSS gave a lead to the other health departments the position may not be quite so straightforward. First, the Griffiths report was directed at England; the remit of the inquiry team did not extend to Scotland or Wales. Second, although the sequence of events suggests that Scotland followed the DHSS's lead in implementing Griffiths, the former Minister for Health and Social Work, John MacKay, is on record as saying that the health board chairmen were putting pressure on him to introduce general managers long before Griffiths was thought of (Davies 1986a). Consequently, he alleges it is untrue to see general management as an English solution being foisted on Scotland at the bidding of DHSS ministers. As we reported, the general manager was originally proposed in a Scottish report some 20 years ago. How much of this, if any, influenced Griffiths is an open question but it may be a subtle example of how the traffic flow of ideas and policy themes can be two (or even three) way in Britain and not one way as a top-down model of policy-making and central-local relations would have us believe. Third, officials in the SHHD denied that Scotland had followed the DHSS's lead in any strict sense claiming that the move to introduce general management had actually originated at Cabinet level. 'Once the order went out there should be general managers, well there had to be general managers'. Thereafter, modest differences in approach were adopted across Britain.

The essence of Griffiths was to change the managerial culture of the NHS and to make management more proactive and less reactive (Day and Klein 1983). Whether the specific proposals will succeed in this endeavour remains to be determined. There is some concern, however, that Griffiths' concentration on *hospital*, rather than *health care*, management is somewhat outdated and at odds with current priorities and the community care thrust of current policy. The 1974 NHS reorganisation was designed to achieve integrated care so that primary care and community care services would not remain separate or continue to be overshadowed by the hospital sector. Griffiths appears to have overlooked the significance of integrated care and its importance for the priority care groups. Such a philosophy of care demands a team management approach based on consensus. Concern has been expressed by no less an authority than the Health Advisory Service (HAS) in England and Wales that general management may prove to be inimical to successful community care.

HAS's 1984/85 annual report (Health Advisory Service 1985, page

8) states unequivocally that the introduction of new management arrangements 'is threatening to destabilise existing support structures for services for elderly and mentally ill patients'. Moreover, while multidisciplinary consensus team management may be incompatible with the general management concept, HAS visits 'show the need for many disciplines to continue to be directly involved in the planning and operation of services for elderly or mentally ill people'. It is suggested that 'the spirit of consensus will be lost only at great cost to patients'. If Day and Klein (1983, page 1813) are correct then the Griffiths changes mean moving the NHS from 'a system that is based on the mobilisation of consent to one based on the management of conflict'.

In abandoning multidisciplinary management a narrower emphasis on hospital, as distinct from health care, management is at least a possibility. General managers at all levels in the health service may be reluctant to give much consideration to policy options which 'hive off' responsibility for implementation to agencies outside the service and over which they have no control and restricted influence. Whether this means that NHS planning will become increasingly unilateralist remains to be seen: the signs are that, for a variety of reasons, this may be beginning to occur, particularly in respect of the long-stay hospital closure programme (Wistow and Hardy 1986). Moreover, at national level in England there is further evidence for this view in the structure and membership of the Supervisory and Management Boards. Not only does the DHSS Social Services Inspectorate not have membership on either Board but the Chief Nursing Officer was not in the original membership of the Supervisory Board and was included only after vigorous – and public – lobbying. On the social work side, this is in sharp contrast to the position in Wales (though not Scotland) where the Chief Social Work Service Officer is a member of the Health Policy Board. Nevertheless there remain fears that under the new arrangements in health service management at the centre, social services may suffer and occupy second place in policy discussions. It is acknowledged by Welsh Office officials that to avoid this the social services corner must be fought hard by well placed administrators.

Chapter 3
MAPPING THE ORGANISATIONAL CONTEXT
2   CENTRE-CENTRE AND CENTRE-LOCAL
ADMINISTRATIVE RELATIONSHIPS AND
FINANCIAL ARRANGEMENTS

INTRODUCTION

The Scottish and Welsh Offices are at the hub of two sets of
relationships: centre-centre (the Edinburgh and Cardiff connections
with Whitehall) and centre-local (the Edinburgh and Cardiff connections with local administrative units within their own territories).
Relationships between central and local government have received
growing attention from students of public policy both in England
(Jones 1980; Ranson and others 1985; Goldsmith 1986a and 1986b)
and in Scotland (Page 1980; Rhodes and Midwinter 1980; Keating and
Midwinter 1983; Goldsmith 1986a and 1986b). Relationships in Wales
have received less attention but have not been wholly neglected
(Madgwick and James 1980; Rhodes and Midwinter 1980; Goldsmith
1986a and 1986b). However, of the studies commissioned by the
ESRC panel on central-local relations, only one was explicitly
designed to explore the intra-UK dimension. The studies of individual
service areas were, in effect, focused on the situation in England with
only rare and incidental glances beyond its borders (for example,
Wistow and Hardy 1986).

In the local government field, there was some interest during the
late 1970s in the Scottish system of regional reviews. Some observers
in England viewed them as a potentially valuable mechanism enabling
individual local authorities to relate to the Scottish Office on a more
corporate basis in contrast with the largely separate sets of functional
relationships between English local authorities and the central departments in Whitehall (Stewart 1977; Central Policy Review Staff 1977).
Interest in comparative studies of central-local relations in the social
policy field has, however, been more rare, if not non-existent
(Williamson and Room 1983). Within the health field, studies of
central-local relations have been virtually confined to England (Elcock
and Haywood 1980; Haywood and Alaszewski 1980; Ham 1981;
Nicholls 1981; Allen 1982) with limited comment on Scotland
(Hunter 1979; 1980) and nothing on Wales.

More striking is the virtual absence of analysis of centre-centre

46

relationships, particularly in respect of health and related services. In this chapter, therefore, we seek to sketch in the nature of, and recent developments in, the relationship between Whitehall and Edinburgh and Cardiff, in the context of our case study of community care. We then review and contrast central-local relationships in each of the three mainland countries as expressed in this field of policy.

EDINBURGH-LONDON RELATIONSHIPS

As we noted in Chapter 1, conventional wisdom has it that the lead department for health policy in Britain is the DHSS. Scope for diversity is held to be confined to 'organisational issues or administrative process' and is not to be found in 'functional policies'. Officials in the Scottish Office gave some credence to this view. As one put it:

> It would be unrealistic to expect the goals of society to get out of phase North and South of the Border . . . I think we would all agree it is the way we do things rather than what we are doing or attempting to do that is different.

If, however, there was agreement that the scope for diversity was limited, it soon became clear that the extent of these limits could, in practice, be very broad indeed. Officials did not question that policy in Scotland was orientated towards the growth of community care. Yet the differences in the routes by which the policy was being pursued and in the relative priority accorded to it were such as to question whether the Scottish Office was in reality pursuing the same 'functional policy' as the DHSS or the Welsh Office (see Chapter 4).

Moreover, there were also signs that relations between the Scottish Office and the DHSS were beginning to undergo change of a gradual, if as yet somewhat intangible, nature. In particular, officials noted the growth of a more independent mental set with the result that they were less likely to look South for clearance before taking action.

In the opinion of one official:

> The Scottish Office feels that it's grown up and that's got a lot to do with younger and more lively administrators in key positions now than was the case even 10 years ago. It was an attitude of mind that you couldn't do anything, make a move without finding out if that was alright with DHSS. It was an attitude of mind which was difficult to break down but it is happening now . . . We are increasingly going our own way . . . it's a steady divergence. Basically we have just drifted apart and we have, over the past few years, had a group of people who have been more willing to take initiatives, purely Scottish initiatives, than it appeared our prede-

cessors were and I think, to some extent, this was encouraged by George Younger (former Secretary of State for Scotland) when he established the junior Ministers as being Ministers for such and such. It gave them a status.

To some extent, too, the divergence between London and Edinburgh may be a spin-off from the devolution debate in 1979.

People realised, well, we didn't get devolution, we did have the Scottish Office, let's make the best we can of it.

An identity with Scottish interests long preceded the devolution proposals, however, and set the Scottish Office apart from Whitehall. Thus Kellas (1980) maintains that a nationalist streak has always been present among officials in the Scottish Office and not just because four-fifths of the top civil servants are Scots. All officials working in, or allied to, the Scottish Office.

... soon develop a loyalty to Scotland, which is somewhat different in quality from the loyalty which civil servants in other departments have for their departments. Scotland is a nation, not just an administrative unit, and in a sense the Scottish Office men are nationalists. They argue the case for Scotland ... (page 109).

CARDIFF-LONDON RELATIONSHIPS

The relatively recent transfer from the DHSS to the Welsh Office of responsibilities for health and personal social services has meant that Cardiff has tended to follow the London 'lead' comparatively closely. This position is now changing as the Welsh Office 'comes of age' and grows in experience and self-confidence. Although a particularly recent phenomenon in the health and PSS field, some officials have argued that such developments became apparent in, for example, land reclamation and housing policy as early as the mid 1970s (personal communication). Linked to the switch in responsibilities from Whitehall to Cardiff has been the progression to senior levels of civil servants who had not previously worked in the DHSS. Another factor contributing to the adoption of a more independent line is the opportunity afforded by physical distance from Westminster and Whitehall together with the degree of administrative and, especially, financial devolution which now obtains. Thus it was suggested that there was:

... not very much Parliamentary interest, not much realisation of the extent to which administrative functions have been deconcentrated to Cardiff and the extent to which the Secretary of State does have control over his budget and operation. And that for an administrator is really quite big news. But it is . . . so recent that I don't think people have quite cottoned on. So we do have that little bit of elbow room of the sort which doesn't come very often, I think, in civil departments and home departments.

Given the recentness of these developments, relatively few tangible examples of the Welsh Office's capacity to take an independent line yet exist. The most fully developed in the social policy field is the 'strategy for mentally handicapped people', which we discuss in some detail in Chapter 5. Nonetheless, the very fact that an 'independent thrust' had been developed in one policy field increased self-confidence and encouraged independent reviews of policy for elderly and (at a later date) mentally ill people.

At the same time, however, there were a number of constraints on this process, especially the national framework of service provision and the scarcity of policy planning resources within the Office. The latter imposed upon Cardiff the need to be selective about the areas in which an independent line could be pursued. The DHSS had concentrations of expertise which enabled them to mobilise a team to look at particular problems very much more readily than the Welsh Office. Equally, there were areas of policy where there was no apparently good reason for variations between England and Wales. In the case of child care, for example, where there was a common legal framework, there was no particular reason to suggest that the experience of those operating in the child care field in Wales was markedly different. Generally speaking, therefore, the Welsh Office made 'a conscious decision every time' whether to be content to accept the DHSS lead, perhaps adapting it to Welsh needs, or whether to pursue a more independent line. However, the extent to which the latter course was possible in practice seemed essentially constrained by the volume of expertise and staff resources within the Office.

CENTRAL-LOCAL RELATIONS: ENGLAND

Historically, the DHSS inherited the *laissez faire* tradition of the Ministry of Health in its relationships with local bodies (Griffiths 1966). However, since its emergence in the late 1960s it has sought to develop a more interventionist approach, spurred on in part by a perceived need to promote more equity in the allocation of resources both territorially and between acute medicine and the 'Cinderella' groups. A further factor was the 'planning mood' (Gunn 1976) sweeping through government at this time coupled with what Burns

(1981) refers to as a 'recrudescence of the hard-line managerialism . . . which had manifested itself in America'. Heclo and Wildavsky (1981) call this period of turbulence and reform in the public sector 'the new rationalism'.

The election of a Conservative government in 1979 initially produced a marked change in the stance of the DHSS towards health and local authorities. Particularly while Patrick Jenkin was Secretary of State (1979–1982), the emphasis was upon the 'disengagement' of the Department from the health service to allow greater scope for local decision-making. However, the localist experiment was short lived. Parliamentary pressures to improve accountability (House of Commons Committee of Public Accounts 1981; 1982; House of Commons Social Services Committee 1980) together with a ministerially led emphasis on the need to manage existing resources more effectively resulted in the introduction of more centralised patterns of accountability. Since 1982, annual reviews have been conducted by Ministers of regions and by regions of their constituent districts (see Chapter 4). As we noted in Chapter 2, the introduction of general managers at all levels in the service following the Griffiths report of 1983 has similarly been designed to assist the Department in establishing clear lines of accountability and holding identified managers accountable for performance against agreed objectives. The combination of general management and the review process represents a substantial shift in the style of central-local relations within the NHS, though its effects have yet to become clear.

No such managerial hierarchy of accountability exists in the personal social services. Unlike the NHS, the DHSS does not allocate resources to these services and is thus not directly accountable to Parliament for their use of resources. The Departmental role is, therefore, limited to general guidance and persuasion supplemented to a limited extent by centrally funded initiatives designed to encourage local authorities to adopt national policy objectives, of which there have been increasing numbers in the 1980s (Westland 1981; House of Commons Social Services Committee 1984; 1986). However, its interest in improving performance is reflected in the establishment of a new Social Services Inspectorate out of the previous social work service with a clear remit to assist local authorities in achieving a more cost effective use of resources (DHSS 1983d).

Relationships between Whitehall and the periphery have been undergoing a process of centralisation in the housing and education services no less than in the NHS. The balance of influence between the DES and local authorities has varied over time and Ranson (1984) has identified three periods of dominant interest: the early post-war period in the mid 1950s being characterised by central dominance; the ensuing years up to the early 1970s by local dominance; and the most recent period by an accelerating increase in central control over resources accompanied by a strategy of decentralising greater influence to market/consumer interests. Comparatively speaking, however, the DES has been accustomed to operate in a more promotional, if not directive, mode than the DHSS throughout the post-war period and, in the opinion of Regan (1977, page 35), has more power 'than most government departments today over their respective services'.

Housing services have historically been more centralised than education and Karn (1985, page 163) has argued that 'in housing local authorities have been used to a degree of autonomy not enjoyed in other services. In recent years, however, she suggests that 'this autonomy has been severely eroded' as central government has adopted national housing policies, tolerated less divergence from such policies and, in the most recent period, introduced closer controls over expenditure in a service in which cuts in local government spending have been most heavily loaded. A study of central government departments conducted in the early 1980s largely confirms this view and, in contrast with the DHSS which was then pursuing its 'disengagement' policy towards the periphery, found that DOE officials emphasised the 'steerage role' of the Department towards housing services (Jasp Team 1984).

CENTRAL-LOCAL RELATIONS: SCOTLAND

Each of the three departments in Scotland with which we are concerned – SHHD, SED (SWSG) and SDD – relates to the field in a different way. The relationship between the SHHD and health boards, as we noted in Chapter 2, oscillates between an interventionist and directive stance on the one hand and a detached, *laissez-faire* one on the other. In contrast the SWSG and the SDD have adopted much less obtrusive stances by virtue of the fact that they are dealing with elected local authorities over whom they have little direct influence when it comes to priorities. In the case of the Housing Division it deals with the Housing Corporation and housing associations as well as the 56 housing departments at district and islands council level. The SWSG, through its advisory service, does maintain close contact with the 12 social work departments run by the regional and islands councils although, as the efficiency scrutiny argued, its influence on policy is negligible (Moyes 1985).

In general terms central-local relations in Scotland appear less formal than in England with more reliance at the centre upon informal channels of communication both horizontally among central departments and vertically between central departments and field agencies.

51

This is borne out by work carried out as part of the ESRC's initiative on central-local relations (Goldsmith 1986a and 1986b). Contributing factors include shorter lines of command, fewer actors, and the greater frequency of interpersonal contact. As one senior official commented:

> . . . relations between the Scottish Office and local agencies are very different [from those in England], both procedurally and on a day-to-day basis. We know pretty well everyone in SHHD and in the health service of any significance who is concerned with administering a health board . . . whereas there is no way people in DHSS could do the same. Even for the Regions it must become a bit of a problem.

But it is not simply a matter of scale of operation. The Scottish Office is not really a government department in the way that Whitehall departments are, so comparisons between the two can be misleading. The Scottish Office, like the Welsh Office, takes upon itself tasks of a regional nature in relation to many of its functions, including health, as was pointed out in Chapter 2, which brings it into direct managerial contact with a number of areas of activity.

CENTRAL-LOCAL RELATIONS: WALES

Similar considerations apply in Wales where, for example, the absence of a regional tier of administration for the NHS has been accompanied by a closer involvement in the detail of aspects of health service management. Historically, therefore, the Welsh Office has adopted a less interventionist stance towards local government services than the more directly administered health service. However, in 1979, the incoming Conservative government's philosophy of 'disengagement' appears to have been adopted more uniformly in relation to the latter than the former. Under the previous administration, a junior minister held monthly meetings with health authority chairmen at which operational management matters were discussed, including localised industrial disputes. Paradoxically, however, Ministers lacked the capacity to secure changes in the strategic direction of the health service. Health authorities were able to pay little more than lip service to the 1976 Welsh Office priorities document because there was no effective mechanism for following it through from the centre and for monitoring performance. Detailed intervention ended in 1979 and, for a time, the Welsh Office 'stood back' and encouraged health authorities to 'get on with' managing their own affairs. Subsequently, however, with the introduction of annual reviews and the implementation of Griffiths, the Welsh Office resumed an interventionist role but its orientation was both selective and strategic:

52

... one of the ways in which we choose where to get involved is where, without our intervention, you couldn't bring about changes in the strategic pattern of services, either because of an imbalance between health authorities or between health and social services or another group of authorities ... or because of internal power lobbies within the structure which inhibit change in the sort of direction that the government wants to see change and it can only be achieved from outside.

One example of this stance was the emphasis on investing the half per cent efficiency savings, which health authorities were required to make annually, in priority group services. This had been included in the first (1984) annual reviews and was seen to have been very largely achieved.

In the personal social services, a form of centralised planning survived the 'disengagement' period in the shape of the annual cycle of planning statements (or LAPS). Broadly equivalent to the English system which was disbanded in 1979/80, the Welsh LAPS was consciously retained at this time, in part due to local authority support.

In both health and personal social services, central-local relations tend to be less formal than in England. This is largely due to factors similar to those operating in Scotland: shorter hierarchies, fewer actors and, therefore, closer interpersonal relationships in what are relatively small, if not incestuous, administrative and professional policy communities. As a result, the view from Cardiff was that the DHSS envied the Welsh Office's 'facility of being close to the authorities [they] deal with, of being able to grapple with eight local authorities and nine health authorities, and the impossibility of them, from the centre, being able to do it in England'. This proximity to the field is illustrated by the administrative as well as professional officials taking the policy debate to the local agencies. Two examples of this process are: the role of civil servants in mobilising support among local interests for the All Wales Mental Handicap Strategy: and the willingness of officials to encourage local participation in the construction of a corporate programme for the NHS.

FINANCIAL ARRANGEMENTS FOR INTER-SERVICE COORDINATION

Finance is a crucial consideration in community care, and not merely the adequacy of total resources allocated to this purpose. Equally important is the capacity of the centre to secure a flow of resources between functions. The development of community care has implied a shift in the balance of responsibilities – and therefore in the balance of costs – borne by health and local authorities, respectively. Most particularly, the introduction of new service models has been dependent upon the expansion of personal social services and the acceptance of a commensurately smaller role for hospital services, if not for all forms of NHS provision.

The need to devise financial arrangements which permit such a pattern of service development is, therefore, a common one throughout Britain. However, the arrangements for allocating public expenditure, including local government expenditure, differ in Scotland and Wales from those in England in ways which provide the Scottish and Welsh Secretaries with greater room for manouevre than their counterpart in the DHSS.

While the Social Services Secretary is, in principle, equipped to initiate service policies which span health and personal social services boundaries he is much less able to ensure that resources flow in the same direction. In the early 1970s, the DHSS secured Treasury agreement for proportionately higher growth rates in the personal social services than in the NHS, precisely to underpin the expansion of community care services. And, in practice, the response of local authorities was to increase their spending on personal social services by significantly larger amounts than those anticipated in successive expenditure White Papers, peaking at 19 per cent growth in real expenditure in 1973/4 (Webb and Wistow 1982). Even when tight financial constraints were imposed upon public expenditure following the financial crisis of the mid 1970s, the Department still planned for a more rapid rate of growth in the personal social services than in the NHS (DHSS 1976b). Again the local authorities did better and achieved growth rates in excess of the planning totals (Webb and Wistow 1982). Nonetheless, DHSS aspirations to increase social services provision in ways which complement the Department's policies for community care have increasingly fallen foul of wider financial policies for the reduction of local government expenditure.

The conflict in the basic service objectives of the DHSS and the expenditure containment objectives of the Treasury and the DOE came most sharply into focus in the 1980 Expenditure White Paper. This document not only showed a continuing rate of growth for the NHS but also indicated a greater rate of reduction for personal social services expenditure than any other local authority service (Webb and Wistow 1982). It was the emergence of so apparently fundamental a contradiction between funding and service policies for the NHS and personal social services that largely accounted for the stringent criticisms, made by the House of Commons Social Services Committee (1980), of the lack of policy coherence in the DHSS (see Chapter 2).

In subsequent years, Expenditure White Paper planning totals for the personal social services were increased to permit annual growth rates of 2 per cent, the amount the DHSS considered necessary to permit the maintenance of service levels against the growth of need. In practice, while personal social services spending again exceeded the planning total (in aggregate terms but not in all local authorities), such growth proved inadequate both to maintain *per capita* service levels for the growing numbers of over 75 year olds and to meet increases in need among care groups (Webb and Wistow 1982; 1987).

Nonetheless, even if the DHSS were able to negotiate with the Treasury and the DOE an adequate increase in personal social services spending, further difficulties would quickly arise. Because of the unhypothecated nature of the rate support grant (RSG), none of the central government departments could guarantee that increased resources would find their way into the personal social services rather than some other local government function. Nor is this a purely theoretical consideration: although personal social services spending across England as a whole increased by more than the 2 per cent allowed for in Expenditure White Papers over the four years to 1984/85, some social services departments secured less resources than the national average. Aggregate levels of spending increased by 9.5 per cent over that period, but in the five years to 1985/86 nine departments experienced real cuts. In addition, a further 43 departments received less than the amount which would be needed over that five year period to meet the average of 2 per cent growth annually (House of Commons Social Services Committee 1986, paragraphs 35 and 39). In other words, individual local authorities have been exercising their right (which has been explicitly recognised in successive Expenditure White Papers) to allocate spending between functions in accordance with purely local priorities.

Faced with the twin difficulties created, on the one hand, by the non-congruence of policies for community care and those for local government spending and, on the other, by the non-hypothecated grant system, two limited attempts to square the circle have been initiated by the DHSS: joint finance, which was introduced in 1976 as a form of specific grant, and, since 1983, the direct transfer of resources from health to personal social services via, in effect, an agency payment. However, neither of these mechanisms has been wholly successful. Joint finance has ensured that additional resources top-sliced from the health programme do find their way into social services departments. But they have not always been spent in ways which directly benefit the NHS or, even more particularly, to support projects which enable the transfer of patients from long-stay hospitals to personal social services care. Another limitation of joint finance is

55

that it provides only a source of short-term funding: growth has to be available within local government if joint finance is to generate significant additions to services in the longer term. By contrast, the more recent resource transfer initiative is both directly linked to patient transfers and facilitates long-term health service support. However, early experience suggests that many health authorities are reluctant to transfer resources and that the overall level of funds available may be insufficient to provide adequate alternatives (Wistow and Hardy 1986; Wistow and Fuller 1986). Both of these financial mechanisms, which also apply in different ways in Scotland and Wales, are described more fully in Chapter 7.

In Scotland and Wales the position with regard to financial arrangements is somewhat different, largely as a result of changes to public expenditure procedures made in anticipation of devolution. The Royal Commission on the Constitution (1973) maintained that support for Scottish and Welsh devolution stemmed in large measure from a feeling that there would be advantage in each country being freer to use its total allocation of resources in ways which did not conform so closely to a UK governmental framework. Although, in fact, there proved to be insufficient public support for political devolution (a substantial degree of administrative devolution already existed as we have suggested in Chapter 2), new financial arrangements were put in place with the result that the switching of resources between services is, in principle, easier to achieve in Edinburgh and Cardiff than in Whitehall. The overall level of public expenditure in both Scotland and Wales is, of course, a matter for annual negotiation with the Treasury. Since 1978, it has been allocated under the terms of the 'Barnett formula' whereby a 'fixed proportion of changes in English or English/Welsh expenditure goes to Scotland and Wales' (Kellas and Madgwick 1982, page 23).

In the same year (1978), the services within the Scottish and Welsh Secretaries' programmes were divided into two categories for public expenditure purposes. The smaller of these categories covers the predominantly economic functions (including agriculture, industry, energy, trade and employment) which are primarily influenced by other EEC and UK policies. For this reason, resources are separately provided for each of these services and are not transferable. By contrast, the second category of 'other services' is provided for by means of a block grant within which the Scottish and Welsh Secretaries have discretion to allocate expenditure between individual activities. The block grant accounts for the bulk of all public spending within their control: some 90 per cent and 97 per cent respectively of the 1984/85 Scottish and Welsh programmes (HM Treasury 1984, page 117). On the other hand, it needs to be recognised that this system offers less scope for the Welsh Secretary to reallocate expenditures than is the case in Scotland, since fewer governmental functions, most particularly Home Office matters, are administered directly from Cardiff than from Edinburgh (Kellas and Madgwick 1982, page 24). However, it provides both Secretaries of State with a degree of flexibility in switching resources between functions which is not available to their Whitehall counterpart. In practice, such flexibility exists only at the margins but it allows new resources to be directed to support service policy directions and emphases determined within the two territorial Departments.

The importance of these new arrangements was underlined by the then Scottish Secretary, George Younger, in evidence to the Select Committee on Scottish Affairs in 1980:

> As I understand it, in 1978 there was a change. Certainly I remember on the previous occasion I was in the Scottish Office (1970–74), switching programmes within the Scottish Office's responsibility required Treasury permission. This was not by any means easy to obtain and a great deal of trouble was taken trying to get it. We now have the ability to do this without permission. (Quoted in Kellas and Madgwick 1982, page 25)

On the same occasion he also emphasised that he would not readily wish to return to the earlier arrangements because:

> ... I would have to give up the ability to switch between my individual programmes, and that I do not wish to do, because Scottish needs are often very different; Scottish priorities are often very different. I would not wish to have my priorities dictated to me by my Whitehall colleagues. I now have complete control over those priorities myself. (Quoted in Kellas and Madgwick 1982, page 25)

If, in practice, only marginal shifts in resource allocations are feasible, especially when the growth increment is tightly constrained, Keating and Midwinter (1982) have reported that modest reallocations have taken place in Scotland. In 1982, for example, rather less was allocated to transport and housing and rather more to education and law than in the comparable English or English/Welsh programmes. In Wales, the prime example of the Secretary of State's powers being exercised in the social policy field is in the funding of the strategy for mentally handicapped people. Officials indicated that the flexibility offered by the block vote enabled them to shift resources and switch priorities and was crucial to the design of the strategy. Not only would such an arrangement require Treasury approval in England (which would previously have been the case in Wales), but – as we have already indicated – the DHSS would have lacked the capacity to target such resources onto social services departments as compared with local government finances as a whole.

This factor alone acts as a significant disincentive for the DHSS even to contemplate the transfer of funds from health programmes to local authorities via the rate support grant mechanism. However, in a provision which applies only to Wales, the Secretary of State was given powers under the 1983 Health and Social Services and Social Security Adjudications Act to make payments directly to local authorities to meet the cost of specific services providing care in the community (Welsh Office 1983b). This provision has constituted the statutory basis for routing NHS development funds into new local authority services (education, housing and especially personal social services) for mentally handicapped people which the Welsh Secretary is satisfied have been planned in accordance with the All Wales Strategy (see Chapter 5).

Shifts in the balance of care from health to personal social services can be supported by the Scottish and Welsh Secretaries in a further way not within the control of the Social Services Secretary in England. This capacity is derived from the existence of separate rate support grant machinery for Scotland and Wales, which in Wales is itself a recent development. It was intended that this machinery should be an integral feature of the financial arrangements accompanying Welsh devolution. Although initially shelved following the failure of the referendum in 1979, the proposal was subsequently resurrected by the incoming Conservative administration and came into effect in 1981/2 (Rhodes and others 1983).

The essential consequence of there being separate RSG arrangements for Scotland and Wales is that the planning totals for expenditure on individual local government services can more readily reflect service priorities within the Scottish and Welsh Offices. As with the allocation of the block grant, the same minister is responsible both for determining the direction of policies for service development and the allocation of the resources needed to fund them. In Wales this power has been used since 1981/82 to reverse the reductions in personal social services planning totals which had been inherited from Whitehall when the separate Welsh RSG negotiations were established. Whereas, in England, actual spending on these services has continued to exceed RSG planning totals, the planning total in Wales has been increased (partly in support of community care policies) to a point where it now exceeds actual spending. As a result, financial and service policies are more mutually reinforcing than in England. The task for the Welsh Office has become, therefore, one of encouraging local authorities to increase, rather than rein in, spending on personal social services in support of policies spanning health and personal social services boundaries. Since, in practice, this implies county councils reallocating resources from education to personal social services, there remain powerful financial barriers to implementing such policies at local level. Nonetheless, a marginal shift towards PSS has taken place in contrast to the English experience. Whereas actual expenditure on PSS in England fell from 9.5 per cent in 1980/81 to 9.3 per cent in 1985/86 as a proportion of total local authority current expenditure, this reduction compared with an increase from 10.2 per cent to 10.9 per cent over the same period in Wales and a smaller increase from 10.3 per cent to 10.6 per cent in Scotland (HM Treasury 1984).

SUMMARY

We noted in the last chapter differences in the structure of the Scottish and Welsh Offices from each other and from the Whitehall departments. A primary distinction between England, Scotland and Wales would appear to be the diffusion, in the first, of power, authority and interests below Cabinet level. By contrast the Secretaries of State for Scotland and Wales are, in principle, able to oversee – from within the confines of their own bailiwicks and the limits imposed by the Treasury on their overall expenditure – the development of coherent and comprehensive policies which span functional boundaries. A more coherent approach, it might be argued, would be that much more difficult to achieve where the final arbiters on any difference of view are the Cabinet and Treasury rather than a single Secretary of State.

The discretionary powers of the two Secretaries of State to reallocate resources between functions – and thus to put resources behind their own local priorities – is perhaps the most important common element between Scotland and Wales and contrasts markedly with the position of the Social Services Secretary in England. A less tangible, but no less real, influence present in both of the territorial departments is a sense of a shared identity with the interests of small and readily definable populations – a national equivalent of 'city pride'. In Wales there was evidence that this had helped to place service goals alongside, if not above, what might otherwise be more dominant sectional and bureaucratic interests. This was clearly more of a feature of the situation in Wales with a population virtually half that of Scotland and with possibly fewer, and less powerful, interests to appease. There is, for instance, in Wales no local authority as large as Strathclyde Region whose population is almost the size of Wales, and no health authority as large as Greater Glasgow with a population of over one million.

The 'generation gap' between the Scottish and Welsh Offices may also be an element in the different atmospheres and operating styles which are evident in the two countries. The Scottish Office, over 100 years old, has the appearance of being ever so slightly care worn and world weary in contrast to a certain youthful exuberance that appears to permeate the Welsh Office perhaps anxious to make its mark through innovations in policy. Of course it may always have been thus and age may be a less significant factor than either the origins of the two Offices – the Scottish Office emerged from the Home Office and the SHHD in particular administers many Home Office functions in Scotland – or the national character of the Scots and the Welsh. We have not pursued the latter in this commentary but it is a feature to be borne in mind in assessing the impact of intra-Britain variations in policy.

Although we detected a growing tendency in Edinburgh and Cardiff to question rather than automatically follow Whitehall initiatives in health and personal social services matters, we were confronted with the more fundamental question of how far, in practice, the Scottish and Welsh Offices actually *make* policies which diverge substantively from those developed by the DHSS.

To illuminate if not solve this puzzle of apparent policy diversity in a unitary state we go on to review policies for community care in general and for mentally handicapped people in particular. Our aim is to explore the extent of, and departure from, policy uniformity which, according to conventional wisdom, is the paramount feature of relationships between Whitehall/Westminster, Edinburgh and Cardiff. We also seek to go further and to identify how far, if at all, variations in policy output are associated with the variations in structural and financial arrangements which have been the subject of this and the last chapters. It is to these matters that we now turn.

Chapter 4
MAPPING THE POLICY CONTEXT: PRIORITIES,
PLANNING AND COMMUNITY CARE POLICIES

INTRODUCTION

Policies to promote community care in Britain have been associated
with three particular elements of strategies for the health and personal
social services: the respective emphases on priorities, systematic
rational planning, and inter-agency collaboration. Each of these
matters was the subject of a central government initiative launched in
the mid 1970s at least in part as a means of attaining community care.

At the same time, perhaps the most fundamental characteristic of
that broader objective has been its multi-faceted and contested nature.
The concept of community care, notwithstanding its imprecision,
implies a shift in the balance of care from institutions to community
facilities, and from health to social services. It also implies a shift in
resources both within health services, and between these and social
services. Finally, it requires a collaborative response from a variety of
separate agencies. As was pointed out in Chapter 1, this is necessary at
three levels – national, local and field.

Controversy has ranged at each level over the *meaning* of community
care, the *motives* for its adoption by successive governments, and its
implications for the allocation of responsibilities between different
public agencies, non-statutory organisations and family, particularly
female, carers. None of these features of community care has
remained constant: for example, the motives for particular initiatives
have included differing blends of social concern, public outrage, and
financial economy.

In exploring the extent of policy uniformity in community care
within Britain, therefore, we need to take into account variations in
the emphases associated with the strategy, not only over time but also
between England, Scotland and Wales. It is necessary to establish, for
example, whether community care has held the same meaning and
implications for the allocation of service responsibilities in each of the
mainland territories during particular periods. In addition, we shall
consider whether there have been any significant variations in means
as well as ends: that is, in the nature of the principal instruments
adopted for the implementation of community care in each country.
One group of instruments, the various mechanisms devised to

61

promote inter-agency collaboration at local level, are the focus of Chapters 6 and 7.

In this chapter we concentrate on the approaches to planning and priorities adopted by the central departments in each country. An account of the evolution of community care as a general thrust of policy then follows for each country. In Chapter 5, we conduct a more detailed exploration of variations in the strategies adopted towards mentally handicapped people, the client group which has been the focus of both the earliest national client group plans and also some of the most recent policy developments in this field.

First, however, it needs to be emphasised that policy initiatives do not take root in virgin soil. They have to find space to grow amidst the accretion of inherited policies. Existing infrastructures of services, spending patterns and interest groups all have an impact upon the shape of new policy initiatives and may crucially determine their outcome. For this reason, we begin by reviewing patterns of spending and service provision for the health and personal social services in England, Scotland and Wales including a brief comment on the growing private sector in the social care field.

SERVICE AND RESOURCE PROFILES

a. *National Health Service*

There are quite striking differences in health expenditure levels between England, Wales and Scotland with the Celtic fringe receiving a larger proportion of expenditure on health than England. *Per capita* spending on health services in Scotland in 1982/83 was 25 per cent higher than in England and 20 per cent higher than in Wales. The differential has widened over the years (see Table 1); for example, for hospital and community health services, Wales has gradually moved from a position of 'under-funding' compared with England in the latter half of the 1970s to very slight 'over-funding' in terms of 1984–85 expenditure. Family practitioner services, on the other hand, have been consistently above the level in England and Scotland. Birch and Maynard (1986) confirm that the differences between countries have widened since they last looked at the position in 1980. According to the Central Statistical Office (1986), Scotland accounts for a larger share of national expenditure than its population share while Wales accounts for a proportionate share. The regions within England are as diverse as the constituent parts of the UK. The additional resources in Scotland are largely utilised to maintain a hospital service which is considerably larger than its English or Welsh counterparts (Cole and others 1985) while the community health service and primary care

62

Table 1   Health services expenditure 1979/80 and 1982/83: Great Britain*

1979/80	Total £m	Per capita £	Hospital services	% Proportion allocated to: Community health services	Family practitioner services
England	7,341.1	158	59.1	6.1	21.7
Wales	461.8	166	57.9	6.4	23.0
Scotland	1,020.1	198	61.9	5.6	18.0
1982/83					
England	11,425.9	243	58.2	6.4	22.7
Wales	737.8	262	57.0	6.5	23.6
Scotland	1,588.8	308	62.3	5.8	18.6

*Central administration, other services and capital expenditure percentages of total have been omitted.

Sources: Central Statistical Office. Regional Trends 17 and 20, 1982 and 1985. London, HMSO.

sectors are smaller in proportionate terms. The Scottish health service is dominated by the hospital sector and to maintain it there is a higher volume of resources in terms of medical and nursing staff and beds. There are, for example, 41 per cent more hospital medical staff per 100,000 population in Scotland than in England; Scotland also has the highest number of beds available (Cole and others 1985).

Bed availability in NHS hospitals was highest in Scotland in 1979 with 11 beds available per 1,000 population for all specialties (see Table 2). The rate was 3 per 1,000 more than the average for the UK as a whole and more than 2 per 1,000 higher than for any English region or for Wales. In 1983, Scotland again had an average or above average proportion of expenditure devoted to hospital services. There were 11.1 beds available in NHS hospitals per 1,000 population in Scotland, a higher figure than in any English region or Wales. Scotland also had the highest rate for occupied beds per 1,000 population. Generally bed stays are longer in Scotland than elsewhere (McGuire 1985). This could reflect medical practitioners' preferences or an absence of alternative provision in the community, although this absence could itself reflect longer hospital stays. Birch and Maynard (1986) argue that Scotland appears to be doing less with the resources available to it than England and while this may reflect a higher quality of care the available evidence does not allow a judgement to be made one way or the other.

Table 2   NHS hospitals: numbers of beds 1979 and 1983

	Numbers per 1,000 population					
	Available beds		Occupied beds		Discharges and deaths	
	1979	*1983*	*1979*	*1983*	*1979*	*1983*
England	7.9	7.3	6.3	5.9	116.4	128.5
Wales	8.4	8.0	6.5	6.3	126.0	132.9
Scotland	11.3	11.1	9.4	9.1	142.4	141.1

Sources: Central Statistical Office. Regional Trends 17 and 20, 1982 and 1985. London, HMSO.

If an attempt is made to reconcile expenditure with policy objectives the conclusion reached by a group of health economists (see Cole and others 1985) is that the sought after shift from general and acute hospital services towards long-term care of the elderly, the mentally handicapped and the mentally ill has not taken place. 'Distribution of resources appears to have been determined by historical patterns. This must, to some extent, call to account the planning process' (McGuire 1985). In other words a strategy of *policy maintenance* has been pursued rather than one of *policy change* as implied in the national statement of priorities, *SHAPE* (SHHD, 1980b).

These trends are not apparent in Wales where the balance of provision is much closer to that in England although, as noted above, *per capita* spending on health services is slightly higher. However, in its approach to community care and to mental handicap services in particular (see below), Wales displays significant differences from England and Scotland.

b. *Personal social services*

Significant differences in *per capita* expenditure on personal social services are also to be found in England, Wales and Scotland. As with spending on health services, the highest level of spending per head is in Scotland (see Table 3). In 1982/83, net current *per capita* expenditure in Scotland was 19 per cent higher than in England and 32 per cent above that in Wales. Spending differentials remained largely unchanged over the period 1979/80 and 1982/83, though England and Wales obtained marginally smaller increases in spending per head (49 per cent and 44 per cent respectively compared with 51 per cent in Scotland). Part of the differential is accounted for by the inclusion of the probation service within the Scottish social work departments in the 1968 reorganisation. In England probation is a separate service.

after 1974 was a responsibility for *health*, and not merely *hospital*, care. Since the hospital service accounts for around 70 per cent of total expenditure on the NHS, it is no easy task trying to widen the service's sphere of influence. Planning was to provide the necessary framework to enable progress to be made in this direction.

a. *England*

Health planning was put on a more explicit and systematic footing in 1976 with the appearance of the DHSS's consultative document on priorities for the health and personal social services (DHSS 1976b). As it candidly acknowledged, this was 'the first time an attempt has been made to establish rational and systematic priorities throughout the health and personal social services' (page 1). The document also emphasised 'the crucial importance of joint planning' (page 2) at local level if this national strategic overview was to bear fruit in terms of improved services for the priority groups. More specifically, it set differentially higher growth rates for personal social services as against health services and for the priority groups compared with acute and maternity services. At the same time, targets were restated for the provision of various kinds of services.

These priorities, with their far reaching implications for local government as well as the NHS, were broadly accepted within the NHS, although it could not be claimed that a total consensus existed at all levels or among all professional groups. A major concern was whether the desired switch in resources could be achieved to the extent indicated in view of the limited growth rate of revenue for the NHS as a whole at this time.

Following the period for consultation on the 1976 priorities document, revised guidance was issued in 1977 (DHSS 1977b) which attempted to take on board the main criticisms of the earlier document. This stressed that the key to achieving the planned switch in resources from acute services to services for the priority groups, which involved a large investment in community care, was to be found in getting better value for money already allocated. This theme has infused all subsequent central guidance and priorities statements.

There were sharp differences in the approach and style of the two priorities documents and it is worth noting these in some detail because they reveal something of the true nature of (and tension underlying) centre-periphery relations in the NHS and the futility of adhering to a simple and rigid dichotomy between policy-making (the centre's business) on the one hand and implementation (the periphery's business) on the other. In particular, the specificity of the 1976

73

document with regard to service norms and targets gave way in the 1977 document to a less prescriptive, more flexible approach.

This shift in the stance assumed by the DHSS in large measure reflected the reality of central-local relations in the NHS. As Klein (1983a, page 128) explains:

> ... given the principle of infinite diversity (no two populations or communities are the same, no two consultants practice the same kind of medicine, and thus national norms inevitably have to be adapted to unique, local circumstances), the department could not impose such norms irrespective of local circumstances. On closer inspection, the DHSS's apparently solid policy targets dissolved under the acid of reservations.

While the 1976 document conceded that the adoption of national norms could not proceed uninfluenced by local factors, the 1977 guidance went further and made it clear that the expenditure objectives 'were not specific targets to be reached by declared dates in any locality'.

Commenting on the divergence between the two documents, Brown (1977, page 812) argues that whereas the first document 'gave a clear sense of direction about the need to alter priorities' within a given timescale, the later document 'was toned down from firm targets to hopeful aspirations'. He concludes that 'the implications of the change from a prescriptive to a concessionary tone are clear enough', in particular the fact that what was proposed in the 1976 document 'was not acceptable to the health authorities . . .'

The *laissez-faire* flavour of the 1977 guidance on priorities and plans was far more pronounced in the DHSS's 1981 handbook of policies and priorities (DHSS 1981b); indeed, it became the main ingredient. The handbook appeared at a time when Ministers had deliberately set out to disengage themselves (and the DHSS) from the running of the NHS and had sought to move away from *dirigiste* planning and towards the encouragement of local initiative and responsibility. Priority-setting was to be a matter for local decision and local action.

In keeping with this approach, the handbook expressed central government guidance in less detailed and precise terms than either of the previous priorities documents. The broad policies remained the same but were no longer expressed in terms of targets for service levels or financial allocations. As Klein (1985) has noted, there were no longer to be any benchmarks against which to measure progress towards national policies and priorities. However, this localist experiment proved to be short-lived. Treasury and parliamentary pressure to improve accountability (House of Commons Committee of Public Accounts 1981; House of Commons Social Services Committee 1980) resulted in a ministerially led emphasis on the need to manage existing resources more effectively, and in a more interventionist strategy which manifested itself in the introduction of the more centralised patterns of management and accountability described in Chapter 2. As part of this process there are, at the time of writing, discussions within the DHSS about the production of a corporate national plan for the NHS. The plan, which has emerged in embryo, is potentially seen as providing 'another weapon in the armoury of proving that the NHS is now more accountable, more efficient, and under control' (Halpern 1986b, page 648; see also Halpern 1986a).

Increasingly, therefore, Ministers have displayed a growing concern with the fine print of service delivery and a desire to tighten their grip on the NHS. Historically, there is nothing new in the adoption of this position (although the means of realising it are new). The oscillation in centre-periphery relations has been a constant feature of the NHS since its inception and is largely a consequence of the continuing search for the optimum balance between the extremes of centralisation and local delegation (Hunter 1983a).

Through a variety of means, but particularly through the annual performance review system whereby DHSS ministers and civil servants discuss local plans and priorities with each health region, the Department has begun to exercise greater control over health authorities. The objectives of the review system are: to ensure that resources are being allocated in accordance with government policies; to review progress against agreed plans and objectives; and to assess performance in the use of resources (DHSS 1983a, page 31). The Griffiths reforms, as already mentioned in Chapter 2, have reinforced these trends. The performance reviews have served to reintroduce, albeit via a different route, a greater element of central involvement in health planning and priority setting. To some extent, and it remains to be seen how far exactly, the review procedure has replaced central involvement in planning by circular and consultative document. It also remains to be seen how successful the review procedure will prove to be. Day and Klein (1985a, page 1677) believe that 'the development of a system for defining objectives at a national level, and for assessing performance at operational level, promises to bring about the most important transformation in the history of the NHS'.

Despite all this activity focused on strengthening health service management, the policies and priorities remain much the same in terms of favouring the continuing care groups and, wherever possible, providing services for them in the community rather than in hospital (DHSS 1983a, page 11). The DHSS continues to depend, therefore, on complementary developments by local authorities to achieve its policies for the health service. Yet, increases in central control over

75

local government have been concentrated almost exclusively on the resource side and, in effect, have made it more difficult for local authorities to make the contribution expected of them. The criticism of the DHSS by the House of Commons Social Services Committee for its apparent lack of a coherent strategy for health and personal social services particularly noted that 'the need to make short term savings in personal social services budgets may be obstructing the shift to community care' (House of Commons Social Services Committee 1980).

As we mentioned earlier, in England this fundamental incompatibility between the centre's policies for the NHS and local government remains a fundamental barrier to implementing community care. Short of adjusting policies towards local government finance as a whole, there appear to be only two means by which this deadlock might be broken: to channel resources from the DHSS to local government outside the rate support grant mechanism through, in effect, some form of direct grant arrangement; or more separatist planning by the health service resulting in its assumption of responsibilities which the DHSS has hitherto expected local authorities to take up.

This state of affairs is a far cry from that anticipated when the DHSS implemented the 1974 NHS reorganisation and produced the original priorities document of 1976. Then the objective was for NHS planning to interlock with that for the personal social services at both the centre and the periphery. As early as 1972 a ten year planning system was introduced for the personal social services. The Department announced its intention

> ...to develop both for the new health authorities and for local authority services, arrangements for formal planning which will provide for annual reviews by both types of authority, will enable them to draw their plans into relationships with one another, and enable local government and central government jointly to review ... the development of services... (DHSS 1972a, paragraph 5)

The introduction of an equivalent planning system for the NHS was delayed until 1976, by which time the social services planning system had been abandoned – after only one round in 1973 – due to the substantial reduction in forecasts of local government expenditure (Webb and Wistow 1986). A less elaborate three year system of planning statements was introduced in 1977 (Booth 1979) but this survived only two rounds before being cancelled in the wake of the incoming Conservative administration's policies to reduce local government spending. This remains the position and there is therefore no mechanism by which the DHSS can review planning developments for the personal social services alongside those for the NHS. The NHS planning system does remain in place, however, although it was simplified in 1980 following the implementation of the proposals contained in *Patients First* (DHSS and Welsh Office 1979) which heralded a second major reorganisation, and was reinforced by the annual review process described earlier. The former Permanent Secretary at the DHSS has argued that while the 'shine has gone off the word "planning" ... a planning system is essential ... if the DHSS and health authorities are to make sense of public consultation, and the monitoring of performance, in relation to the policy objectives of the service' (Nairne 1985, page 123).

b. *Scotland*

In Scotland a planning *approach* was favoured in contrast to a planning *system* (McGirr 1984). The principal focus of NHS planning in Scotland is the Scottish Health Service Planning Council which, as mentioned earlier, emerged from the 1974 reorganisation. It has no counterpart in England or Wales although the Welsh Office came close to introducing a similar body at the time of the second NHS reorganisation in 1982 (see subsection c below).

The Scottish Health Service Planning Council is an independent advisory body. It advises the Secretary of State at his request or on its own initiative and is obliged to keep under review the development of the health service in Scotland. The Council is not part of the SHHD but has close links with it, and in particular with its Planning Unit, (see Chapter 2).

The committees and working groups of the Council fall into three broad categories: those concerned with programmes of health care for particular client groups; those concerned with the services provided by the different professions; and those concerned with the planning of scientific, technical and non-clinical services. In 1975 a Working Party on Health Priorities was established to give an overview of the health service in Scotland (see below). Multidisciplinary programme planning groups are constituted, as required, to deal with specific client groups such as the elderly, the mentally handicapped and so on.

The most important report from the Council to date is *Scottish Health Authorities Priorities for the Eighties* (*SHAPE*) (SHHD 1980b) which differs substantially from its English counterpart, *Care in Action*, published a year later in 1981. The differences do not lie in the priorities to be pursued but in the presentation of these and in the commitment at national level to their success. Moreover, *SHAPE* broke new ground by showing what might be achieved with three different growth rates in NHS funding.

77

SHAPE was preceded by an earlier priorities memorandum, *The Way Ahead* (SHHD 1976), with which the Planning Council had some involvement. The Council had appointed the Working Party on Health Priorities to review health priorities and *SHAPE* represented the culmination of its efforts; the working party had only modest input into *The Way Ahead*.

The memorandum was a slim (barely 23 pages) version of both the DHSS's 1976 priorities document and the Welsh Office's counterpart published in the same year. It was also the first attempt at national level in Scotland to come to grips with health service priorities although, as Gray and Mooney (1982, page 228) have argued, the document 'amounted to little more than a reflection of the then current thinking, in a very subjective way, about deficiencies in the service'. The document lacked rigour and, unlike its DHSS counterpart, did not include service norms and targets to give a lead to local decision-making.

The Way Ahead was 'about priorities, about the changes necessary to make the best possible use of our resources in a period of severe financial constraint' (SHHD 1976, paragraph 3, page 3). The implication was that, because of reduced or static growth rates in health care spending, priorities should be explicitly set out and adopted. In keeping with the English and Welsh statements, the Scottish memorandum emphasised the need to promote community care through improved primary care and community health services; to lessen the growth rate of the acute sector in order to finance developments in the priority groups; and to promote health prevention and education. Although the need for health board consultation with local authorities is briefly mentioned in *The Way Ahead* it does not receive the prominence it was getting at the time in England. In part this was because the report of the Working Party on Relationships between Health Boards and Local Authorities did not appear until the following year, 1977 (SHHD 1977), which restricted what could be said on the subject in the memorandum.

The principles set out in *The Way Ahead* were closely paralleled four years later in *SHAPE*, an altogether more substantial document and the first really serious attempt in Scotland to determine future priorities for health care. The *SHAPE* report resembled a compendium of a succession of reports on key sectors produced during the six years of the Planning Council's existence by programme planning groups (PPGs) made up of representatives from health, social work and the voluntary sector. It took further the process begun in 1976 and approached the issue of priority setting by offering three possible scenarios based on different resource assumptions ranging from zero growth through $1\frac{1}{2}$ per cent growth per annum to a 3 per cent annual growth rate. An attempt was therefore made to link plans and priorities with likely resource availability.

Fifteen specialty groups, or programmes, were identified and these were banded into three categories – A, B and C. The key community care priority groups all fell within the top priority category A. Revenue expenditure in this category should grow faster than all health service revenue expenditure; category B programmes (including primary dental services, maternity services, general medical services) should grow but at a lower rate than category A programmes; and expenditure on category C programmes (including child health and acute hospital services) should remain almost static in real terms or actually decline – spending on any services in this category should be met from savings. Programmes within each category were not set out in a specific order. However, so far as revenue expenditure was concerned, the greatest emphasis should be given to the prevention of ill-health, services for the elderly (particularly the elderly with mental disability), and services in the community. With regard to capital spending, priority should go to the elderly with mental disability, then the mentally ill, mentally handicapped and the elderly.

The authors of *SHAPE* stressed that they were concerned with 'the national picture' and that 'health boards will properly have the major part to play in determining how expenditure is to be incurred in their respective areas'. While formally true, boards were heavily influenced by *SHAPE* in setting their priorities if for no other reason than the lack of alternative plans and of a planning capability in most boards (see Chapter 6). *SHAPE*, unlike *The Way Ahead* and its English counterpart, *Care in Action*, did contain norms of provision for certain groups like the elderly.

SHAPE also makes it quite clear that:

> ... collaboration in planning and in the sharing of resources between health boards and local authority services is crucial to the success or failure of attempts to achieve the proposed objectives. Failing close collaboration *at every level*, results will continue to fall short of what is attainable ... (SHHD 1980b paragraph vii.i, page 74)

In the light of this statement it is worth noting that *SHAPE* was not a joint SHHD/SED (SWSG) production, unlike both its own PPG reports and the various English and Welsh priorities documents, which were the product of health and PPS interests, but a solo SHHD effort (it is currently under review by an *interdepartmental* working group with the SHHD taking the lead through the Planning Council). An official explained:

> *SHAPE* was only ever intended to be advice to health boards. It was national guidelines for the development of the health service and it was unreasonable for social work authorities to get excited about *SHAPE*'s references to social work provision because they were only ever intended to point up that the health service is not providing a service in isolation.

Because services for, say, the elderly are interdependent and cross agency boundaries

> *SHAPE* in the interests of honesty and accuracy couldn't ignore those but it was not saying, in the same way that it said there should be 40 beds per 1,000 aged 75 and over in the health service, that there should also be so many places or whatever in social work services, or housing. It was just saying that these cannot be ignored in the equation . . . but people got terribly excited about this as if in some way *SHAPE* was asking social work authorities to do things without them being represented on the working group that drew it up.

Social work departments took the view that they ought to have been consulted, via SWSG, in the preparation of *SHAPE* when it clearly contained implications for their services. Significantly, the SHHD working group currently revising *SHAPE* has two social work representatives on it though no one from housing or other services. The reason for social work representation is

> . . . we want to encourage joint planning . . . because the days of separate planning must obviously be over.

Also, as another official commented:

> I think maybe the fact that we've been trying to push joint planning and cooperation generally for a long time has made us think that maybe we don't do it all that well ourselves and we ought to put our own house in order as well as encourage other people to do it and I think we're doing that now.

SHAPE was very much a product of the Planning Council's operating style and approach to planning which may explain the fact that in some ways the report was curiously out of step with the *laissez-faire* spirit of the times. Paradoxically, the skeletal 1976 memorandum was better suited to the period while *SHAPE* would not have been out of place alongside the English and Welsh 1976 documents. In the event, as we have already mentioned, *SHAPE* proved to be very different in tone and substance from its DHSS counterpart, *Care in Action*.

SHAPE was a curious document, indeed something of an oddity, if only because nothing that the SHHD had done up until then logically paved the way for it – it did not represent a natural progression from anything beyond the Planning Council's mode of operation. *The Way Ahead* was a document much more typical of SHHD's traditional operating style which is marked by a 'hands off' relationship with health boards notwithstanding the occasional, and often unpredictable, crisis intervention dictated by political circumstances. It was, in fact, a style which was manifest throughout the NHS in Britain for a short period in the late 1970s and early 1980s (see above).

Central monitoring of *SHAPE* has been hesitant and inconclusive. Its impact on events appears to have been minimal but it is hard to be sure because, unlike the annual performance reviews in England, no publicity surrounds the monitoring exercise which has opted for a lower profile. A year after *SHAPE* appeared, the SHHD issued a circular setting out its approach to monitoring the progress of health boards towards implementing the stated priorities (SHHD 1981). Boards were required to submit priorities statements within a year including a programme analysis of expenditure for the financial year in question, 1981/82. Although the basis of the monitoring exercise was a series of statistical analyses of health boards' returns, they were to be supplemented by two-yearly meetings between each board's chief officers and Departmental teams. Ministers do not become involved in these exchanges as they do in England. The first round of monitoring was completed by the end of 1985. Arrangements for the second round of monitoring are set forth in a further circular (SHHD 1986c) which proposes departmental meetings with all boards over the next two years to review their revised planning statements which take *SHAPE* as their basis.

The response by health boards to the monitoring exercise has been mixed. In part this may be a reflection of the fact (little understood apparently by some people in the SHHD) that, in the words of one civil servant, 'only one or two boards had any sort of planning effort at all in 1980 that went beyond the concept of capital planning'. *SHAPE*'s emphasis on service planning 'required a much more radical redirection of effort within health boards than I think either the Department or health boards had appreciated'. As a consequence a lot of learning took place on both sides. In the case of health boards 'a lot assumed they could draw up their *SHAPE* priorities statement on the back of an envelope and one or two did and they got it back pretty sharpish . . .'. In general the small boards have found little difficulty in producing agreed priorities statements; the teaching boards, however, have experienced great difficulty in reconciling their existing commitments with the shift required to move towards national priorities. To

81

date, the SHHD has met the ten health boards that have produced priorities statements and 'put more or less pressure on them to develop their services in different directions'.

The remit of the interdepartmental review group is twofold: first, to review the *SHAPE* recommendations in the light of progress being made by health boards towards their implementation, of current developments, and of anticipated changes in demand; second, to prepare a revised set of guidelines covering the period up to 1992 which will include some reference to monitoring arrangements. As an official explained:

> ... the objective in looking at SHAPE again is to try and measure that trend to see where it's going to end up against demographic changes and such like and to think whether there's any need to rejig the priorities to give more emphasis to some programmes or more emphasis to services within programmes. The acute sector as a whole has a low priority but should, for example, orthopaedics have a higher priority and if so how do you, whether from the Department or the health board, arbitrate in this perpetual war between consultants and take resources away from the ENT people and give it to the orthopaedics people?

Service planning in social work is virtually absent at national level – a capital building programme represents the only planning that exists. The assessment and communication of priorities to local authority social work departments is handled informally and great reliance is placed upon the advisory service's contacts with the field. There is no counterpart in local authority social work departments to the ten year plans which health boards are being asked to produce (discussed in Chapter 6). Formal expressions of social work views on priorities have been transmitted through the Health Service Planning Council's PPGs. Indeed, as we reported in Chapter 2, an absence of planning and policy analysis within the SWSG is a major criticism of its work.

c. *Wales*

Health planning in Wales has broadly followed developments in England. A planning system, based on an annual planning cycle, was introduced in 1975 with a commitment to comprehensive planning, to programmes of care, to the issuance of central guidelines, and to the preparation of strategic and operational plans by health authorities (Welsh Office 1975).

According to officials, the original planning system was not effective and what emerged from it was negligible. Programme planning teams were set up to produce guidance on priorities (see below) but this was never implemented because the Welsh Office lacked the mechanisms to ensure compliance. In particular, no monitoring was built into the planning system. What is referred to as 'a fairly good planning system on the local authority side' (see below) is only now developing in respect of health services. A revised strategic planning cycle was launched in 1982/83 and health authorities have been submitting their strategic plans for approval by the Welsh Office. The plans will run on a five year cycle for update and a ten year forward look with annual submissions of operational programmes which will form the basis of the annual reviews (see below) to monitor progress.

One official described the Welsh Office's faith in, or realistic appraisal of, the planning system as follows:

> We've got a sort of belt, braces and piece of string approach to planning. We don't just rely on the planning system to deliver the Secretary of State's policies and priorities. We've got all sorts of other disciplines to ensure that we get the stated development in the services that we frankly doubt that the health authorities left to their own devices would deliver.

An annual review system, introduced in 1982, is one such discipline – in part 'just a political kneejerk' to the creation of an annual review system in England 'although we were moving along that line'. The reviews are not just directed towards getting more out of existing services but are intended to make sure that what is released through increased efficiency is channelled towards the priority care groups. They are to be recipients of the first 0.5 per cent of efficiency savings to be achieved each year.

At one stage it looked as though the Welsh Office might pursue a different approach to health planning. In the 1982 reorganisation there was speculation in the consultation document (Welsh Office 1980) on the setting up of an advisory Welsh Health Council along the lines of the Scottish Health Service Planning Council. It was envisaged that such a body would advise the Secretary of State and take a lead role in strategic planning. The proposal was rejected and in its place a series of formal meetings between the Minister and health interests was introduced in 1982 known as the All Wales Health Forum. The Forum has no fixed membership – representation varies according to the topic under discussion. It is intended to provide for the public airing of health issues affecting the Principality to ensure the widest possible debate. At its first meeting the Forum considered the report of the All Wales Working Party on Services for Mentally Handicapped People (Welsh Office 1982).

The first national statement of health priorities for Wales appeared in a 1976 document that in most respects resembled the DHSS statement (Welsh Office 1976) although it also resembled the Scottish memorandum in the absence of service norms and guidelines. Welsh Office officials were somewhat dismissive of its impact. It had 'a very checkered history' and lasted for about six months.

> It stated priorities, those priorities were expounded to the various authorities and they acknowledged them and then took no action on them and still poured their money into acute services.

The emphasis on community care, a feature of the 1976 document, was later endorsed in a 1981 consultative document, *Care in the Community* (Welsh Office 1981), which was closely modelled on the DHSS version (see next section). There was no Welsh equivalent of the 1977 DHSS guidance on priorities to health authorities nor did the Welsh Office produce a version of the 1981 DHSS handbook of priorities and policies, *Care in Action*. The chief reason for not following suit was that officials did not think the handbook contributed anything new to statements that had already been produced. Moreover, there were very real practical constraints. At the time, the Mental Handicap Strategy, which we describe below, was taking up officials' attention and they concluded that it was better to devote their efforts to a strategy which would make something work than 'find a few more brave words to describe what ought to be'. Although Ministers would have welcomed a Welsh counterpart of *Care in Action*, the resources in terms of manpower to write it were not available. However, the Welsh Office subsequently issued a brief review of policies and priorities for health services (Welsh Office 1985b). The document represents the fruits of the Health Policy Board's attempt to pull together the various policy initiatives which are the basis of the Secretary of State's approach to care. It reaffirms the priorities set out in the 1976 document, although it places an even greater emphasis on the development of community and continuing care services. The Secretary of State points out that the document 'provides the basis for a corporate plan for the NHS in Wales' which will set more detailed objectives and targets and enable the Secretary of State to check progress towards their achievement.

A period of disengagement from the field followed in the late 1970s in keeping with the political ideology at the time and with parallel events in England. However it was quickly acknowledged that such a strategy was not working. As one official said, 'we went so far in disengagement that they (the health authorities) forgot we were here'. A process of re-engagement began in the early 1980s, *pace* England, although officials believe that it would have happened in Wales regardless of developments elsewhere.

On the personal social services side, the Welsh LAPS system was introduced in 1977 at the same time as the English system. It differed slightly in its emphasis and contained, for instance, a client group focus, and elements of review with a commitment to timely feedback to local authorities. Regular annual feedback remains a feature of the system, with a further difference from the English experience being the provision to local authorities of inter-authority comparisons.

The LAPS system has been kept under review and was examined in detail in 1980 by a joint working party whose membership included directors of social services. Their report recommended a marked shift in emphasis.

> We had become increasingly uneasy about the extent to which the forecasts in the fourth final forecast year of the planning statements were actually being delivered. There seemed in fact to be very little relationship between what was actually being delivered in terms of expenditure and activity statistics. So that year was dropped and we shifted the emphasis to a monitoring rather than a forecasting statement and we firmed up the guidance over the sort of things that we expected to see dealt with in the meantime and in particular shifted it towards documenting the impact on policy and practice of public expenditure constraints which local authorities were then beginning to experience.

Unlike the English LAPS system, then, which has been abandoned the Welsh system is very much alive although there is a view that if at all possible it needs to be made more relevant to secure effective centre-periphery relations.

The forward planning of local authority personal social services is at a more advanced stage than the health service strategic planning system which is only just getting under way despite the intentions of the mid-1970s. As mentioned, the Welsh Office is currently preparing a corporate plan for the NHS. The plan will not directly include input from the personal social services since it is an initiative which flows directly from the newly appointed NHS Director, but the key notions of joint planning and community care are expected to figure prominently. The plan will be based on the statement of policies and priorities for health services (but not personal social services unlike the 1976 document) in Wales produced in 1985 and referred to earlier.

COMMUNITY CARE POLICIES: EVOLUTION AND EMPHASIS

In this section we review the evolution of community care policies and their varying emphases in England, Scotland and Wales. Some of the underlying principles of the community care initiative are common to

85

all three countries and to avoid unnecessary repetition we consider them in the subsection on England.

a. *England*

The need to adjust the balance of care to enable the continuing care groups to live within the community wherever possible was a central theme in the priorities documents of the mid 1970s. There has been a long established presumption that this policy of community care will produce an enhanced quality of life for the priority groups. In addition, community care has long appealed to governments concerned with cost containment: it has been considered not only better for the client but also, by happy chance, cheaper for the public sector.

As long ago as 1956 the Guillebaud report on the cost of the health service argued the case for promoting community care on both 'humanitarian and economic grounds' (Ministry of Health 1956, paragraph 647). The Mental Health Act of 1959 advocated a substantial expansion of community services for mentally ill and mentally handicapped people, largely on the grounds of providing better and more appropriate standards of care. In the case of mental illness, this shift away from the long-stay hospital was, in part, 'practice-led' in the sense that newly available drugs made it possible for larger numbers of people with a mental illness to live outside hospital settings. The interests of individuals in need were also prominent as motives for the expansion of local authority health and welfare services under the ten year plans called for by the Ministry of Health in 1962. Published in 1963 under the title *Health and Welfare: the Development of Community Care* (Ministry of Health 1963), they were subsequently revised in 1966 by which time client welfare rather than resource scarcity was apparently prominent in the Ministry's thinking. Thus community care was defined as a guiding principle according to which services would be 'designed to meet the needs of people who will wish, whether in sickness or health, to live wherever possible in their own home' (Ministry of Health 1966, paragraph 3).

Perhaps not surprisingly, however, a somewhat different balance between Guillebaud's 'humanitarian and economic' factors seemed to become evident in the mid 1970s as resource constraints became tighter. In the 1976 priorities document, community care took its place alongside the pursuit of other 'low cost' alternatives such as reducing average lengths of hospital stay. Ironically, hard evidence that community care is cheaper has been hard to come by, as the DHSS was compelled to admit to Parliament in 1980 (House of Commons Social Services Committee 1980). The following year, a

DHSS study, conducted under the aegis of the Policy Strategy Unit, concluded that:

> ...for some people community-based packages of care may not always be a less expensive or more effective alternative to residential or hospital provision, particularly for those living alone. In some cases, the community alternative might only appear cheap because its level of provision could be considered inadequate (DHSS 1981c, paragraph 3.27, page 29).

The study further suggested that 'the cost effectiveness of these packages often depends on not putting a financial value on the contribution of informal carers' (paragraph 1.6, page 3).

While there has been extensive agreement on the desirability, from the client perspective, of properly resourced community care policies, there has been no equivalent consensus about what precisely the policy means should be – either in terms of the service packages to be offered or the philosophies of care which should underpin them. Instead of common values and shared understandings, competing models of care exist, each usually reflecting the particular values and interests of individual professional groupings. Models of care based on health, housing and personal social services jostle alongside each other and also alongside different views of the balance to be struck between statutory and non-statutory services. At the same time, the policy has come to have different implications for the overall balance of services depending on whether it is viewed from a perspective located in the NHS or in the personal social services. In the former case, it has traditionally meant shifting the centre of gravity from hospital to predominantly local authority residential services: in the latter it has been associated with shifting the centre of gravity from residential to domiciliary and day care (Webb and Wistow 1982). In such circumstances, implementation is necessarily problematic: inter-agency cooperation must be won and cannot be assumed.

The 1981 DHSS study of community care also noted that the term 'seems to mean very different things depending on the context in which it is used' (1981c, paragraph 2.1, page 7). It argued that much of the confusion surrounding its meaning arose because it was used interchangeably as a *description* of services and as *statements of objectives* (paragraph 2.2, page 7). Without pursuing that distinction here, it is also important to note that the emphasis of DHSS policies with regard to community care has changed over time. The emphasis on care *in* the community as an alternative to hospital care has, in recent years, been overlain by an emphasis on care *by* the community.

Although also advocated by Labour Secretaries of State, this approach was most enthusiastically adopted when Patrick Jenkin was

Secretary of State at the DHSS and formal services were explicitly seen as support for the front line efforts of informal carers. The White Paper *Growing Older* (DHSS, Scottish Office, Welsh Office and Northern Ireland Office 1981) illustrates this approach with great clarity:

> ... the primary sources of support and care for elderly people are informal and voluntary. These spring from the personal ties of kinship, friendship and neighbourhood. It is the role of public authorities to sustain and, where necessary, develop – but never to displace – such support and care. Care *in* the community must increasingly mean care *by* the community.

Under Norman Fowler, the 'beatification' of voluntary and informal care (Westland 1981) has been moderated and replaced by a new emphasis on the shared responsibility of public agencies and informal carers for providing care. The revised interpretation of care by the community as 'shared care' (Fowler 1982) is neatly reflected in the title of the most recent DHSS initiative in this field, 'Helping the Community to Care', introduced in 1985.

The interpretation placed by the DHSS on community care policies as they relate to long-stay hospitals has also undergone a parallel shift in emphasis since the early 1980s. It had long been recognised that the reduction in hospital places for mentally handicapped and mentally ill people, which is fundamental to the DHSS's community care policies for these groups (DHSS and Welsh Office 1971; DHSS 1975), might be achieved in two ways: *directly* by the transfer of existing patients into the community; and *indirectly* by preventing the admission of new generations of long-stay patients. In practice, the emphasis in the second half of the 1970s was upon the indirect route to community care, as the DHSS acknowledged in evidence to the House of Commons Committee of Public Accounts (1983b). At the same time, however, the reduction in hospital places has been more modest than intended. As a result, and under the 'Care in the Community' initiative (DHSS 1981b; 1983b), the emphasis has switched to the 'patient transfer' route (Wistow 1983).

This approach has been actively followed through by Ministers using the recently introduced annual review procedure. Consequently, the primary meaning of community care policies in this context has been associated with the transfer of patients from long-stay hospitals to the community to permit the early rundown and closure of such institutions. It is an approach to community care which has, however, been criticised as unbalanced and partial. For example, the House of Commons Social Services Committee argued that:

... the almost obsessive concentration in public policy on 'getting people out of hospital' has sometimes obscured the basic fact that *most mentally ill or handicapped people already live in the community* ... it is vital that the pressing problems confronting those mentally disabled people already living in the community be more fully taken into account in developing policies of community care. (House of Commons Social Services Committee 1985, paragraph 24, pages xv–xvi)

There has, moreover, been considerable scepticism about the motives for this switch in policy. The starting point for the 'care in the community' initiative was stated in the DHSS's 1981 consultative document in the following terms: 'most people who need long-term care can and should be looked after in the community. This is what most of them want for themselves and what those responsible for their care believe to be best' (DHSS 1981b, paragraph 1.1, page 1). However, the initiative was to be accomplished within existing resources, an approach which the House of Commons Social Services Committee regarded as being 'not simply naive ... (but) positively inhumane' (House of Commons Social Services Committee 1985, paragraph 21, page xiv). The initiative has also been resisted by health service unions opposed to 'cuts' in NHS provision. However, while the 'cost-neutral' assumption underlying the 'care in the community' policy may not make possible the funding of community services at an adequate level, it is equally not the intention of the DHSS that resources should be channelled out of services for the dependency groups. Moreover, as DHSS officials would also emphasise, the need to speed up the discharge of individuals from inappropriate hospital settings is urgent if the present generation of hospital patients is to secure any real benefit from community care policies.

A final influence of growing significance for the meaning and substance of community care is the 'normalisation' philosophy which seeks to ensure for dependent individuals the right to live a life as near to the normal as possible (Wolfenberger 1972). Initially most influential in the development of thinking about care for mentally handicapped people (King's Fund Centre 1980), this approach is increasingly beginning to be reflected in the development of services for other client groups. Perhaps the most important elements of this approach are its emphasis on services responding to individuals' needs in ways which respect their dignity and promote their growth and development. The need for services to be provided in the least restrictive possible settings is also a central feature.

In practice, the normalisation philosophy has had two particularly important consequences for community care to date: first, it has focused attention on the values and principles which underpin community care policies and underlined the need for them to be made explicit and consistent; second, it has led to an increasing appreciation of the role and importance of 'ordinary' housing, as opposed to traditional residential services, being located at the core of community care programmes. This has, therefore, been at least partially responsible for a growing – albeit still modest – involvement of statutory housing authorities and voluntary housing associations in the provision of care packages for the dependency groups.

There are differing views over the extent to which the shift towards community care has occurred. The DHSS in its annual report for 1984 claims that steady progress has been made in achieving the various aims for each of these care groups, although it is acknowledged that a long haul lies ahead. 'Progress has not been even thoughout the country and the pressures on services also vary considerably' (DHSS 1984, paragraph 4.76, page 43).

Some commentators, such as Klein (1983a), point to partial success in switching priorities from acute services to the 'Cinderella' sectors, citing in support of this view data supplied by the DHSS to the Social Services Committee in its monitoring of public expenditure on social services. However, much depends on how the figures are calculated, then interpreted and the years to which they apply. There is no reliable way of predicting whether or not a discernible shift in one or two years is the start of a new pattern or merely a temporary aberration or exception. In addition, national figures conceal local differences and even if a change is perceptible nationally, over large areas of the country covering numerous health authorities there may be no evidence of any change on the ground.

The general view, it is fair to say, is that the shift has either been marginal or has not occurred at all. Ham (1985, pages 70–71), for instance, does not share the DHSS's view that progress has been made and maintains that 'in practice the designated priority services have not always received the increased share of resources intended'. He goes on to explain this state of affairs by suggesting that certain key interests within the medical profession have sought to maintain the existing patterns of services and funding. Other reasons why the desired shift may be faltering and uneven are the result of policy ambiguity (community care can mean everything and nothing) and lack of agreement about the policy itself, which, of course, probably accounts for much of the ambiguity. In addition, one of us has demonstrated that on present trends the targets set for developing community mental handicap services will not be met by 1991, the end of the planning period (Wistow 1985). Moreover, Klein (1983a) identifies 'an alliance of indifference' between the medical profession and lay managers to account for the inertia and slow pace of change. One of us encountered this problem in a review of psychogeriatric provision and research needs in Scotland (Hunter and others 1984). There is no conspiracy among the medical profession to deny the priority sectors resources and attention. Rather it is the inevitable consequence of what happens when there is no steady pressure from within services to remedy the situation. Current patterns of provision, then, owe more to historical inheritance than to power politics within the medical profession even if it is the case that on occasion medical dominance among the acute specialties may determine outcomes. In short, unless there is a lobby for change, particularly for such a low status sector, then the called for shift in priorities is likely to remain a somewhat pious hope. The problem of managing change goes well beyond the level of resources *per se*.

Much of the above applies more or less equally to Scotland and Wales. But there are important differences both between them and between each of them and England.

b. *Scotland*

In Scotland, despite the paper stress (in *The Way Ahead* and *SHAPE*) on community care as a cornerstone of national health policy, the actual commitment to such a strategy appears distinctly muted at best and somewhat at odds with it at worst when compared with developments in England and Wales. As we have noted, a more determined shift towards a community care strategy in Scotland in the mid 1970s was inseparable from the response to the changing financial environment which overtook the public sector in the early 1970s and must be viewed in that wider economic context (Gray and Hunter 1983). The pressure to contain, if not reduce, public expenditure in the NHS and elsewhere became caught up with plans to foster selected priority areas which accounted in part for the resulting confusion about both the origins and ultimate purpose of a community care initiative. Was it about reducing expenditure? Or was it about giving a better deal to the priority sectors? There was policy ambiguity and confusion inherent in the initiative from the start which possibly underlay, and accounted for, subsequent events. In April 1985, the former Minister for Health and Social Work, John MacKay, in his address to the Association of Directors of Social Work (ADSW) said that collaboration between authorities in the area of community care was designed to contain costs as well as contribute to the wellbeing of clients.

There are many indications, some subtle others less so, that community care in Scotland lacks the resonance it enjoys elsewhere.

91

At the level of official documentation and published reports, for instance, there is no Scottish equivalent of the *Care in the Community* consultative documents produced in 1981 by the DHSS and by the Welsh Office. These reports heralded significant changes in joint finance arrangements and a renewed commitment to community care through resource transfers. There was simply no debate along these lines in Scotland – changes to the machinery of joint planning and support finance introduced in 1985 were in large measure a response to pressure from outside lobbies, although they represent a curious mixture of positive and negative modifications which seem likely to leave joint working as unsatisfactory as, or possibly even worse than, before. We return to this area of concern in Chapters 6 and 7.

We have shown that in terms of resources (finance and manpower) not only is Scotland better endowed than the rest of the UK but most of these resources have historically been used to maintain large numbers of long-stay beds. This is as true of the other priority groups as it is of the mentally handicapped. Despite the rhetoric of community care the pressure actually to develop alternative forms of provision to long-stay hospital beds is not present to the same extent as in England and Wales. Indeed, a recent decision by one health board, with Treasury and SHHD approval, to spend £16m on the major redevelopment of a 700 bed psychiatric hospital has caused many to ask what has happened to community care. In endorsing the decision the Minister denied that it would have an adverse effect on community care but the revenue implications of running a new hospital complex *and* starting up new community care developments will be significant and may confound the Minister's optimism. In his remarks on collaboration to the ADSW in April 1985 the Minister made little reference to community care as such and commented on residential services which included hospital care. Indeed, although collaboration was mentioned numerous times, community care was explicitly mentioned only once and then in the context of the voluntary sector's input and the special grant initiative on care in the community launched by the SWSG in January 1985.

But the reasons for a quite distinctive service and policy profile in Scotland go deeper than the particular mix of inputs and centre upon divergent professional (primarily medical) views concerning the appropriateness of long-stay beds as a vital component of service provision.

As Martin (1984, page 66) says with regard to community care and the mentally ill in Scotland, it is 'an interesting example of quite substantial Anglo-Scottish differentiation having developed on the basis of variations in professional and administrative attitudes rather than of legislative decisions'. He continues, 'whereas in England a policy of community care has been promulgated but only very incompletely and imperfectly carried through, in Scotland nothing has been promised and virtually nothing achieved' (page 73). The position is perhaps a little more complex than Martin's cryptic remark suggests. As we argued earlier, at one level (possibly a purely rhetorical or symbolic one) health policy in Scotland appears no different from that in England and Wales. A commitment to community care for the priority groups exists explicitly in a variety of official policy statements. It is at the level below this general aspiration of intent that clear differences in policy over community care begin to manifest themselves.

When Martin suggests that the differences evident in Scotland in services for the mentally ill owe more to professional and administrative attitudes than to legislative decisions he could also have been referring to mental handicap services and, though perhaps to a lesser extent, to those for old people.

There has always (at least since the early 1960s when hospital planning began in earnest) been great caution in Scotland among doctors about letting go of beds and embracing community alternatives. This reflects a traditionally stronger emphasis in Scotland on institutional, if not custodial, forms of provision: institutions for the mentally handicapped and other groups all house more inmates than their English counterparts. Martin points out that the 'heavy dependence on hospital care went hand-in-hand with a low level of activity in the local health and welfare services' (page 67). One could be cynical and argue that the maintenance of long-stay beds made it easy for local authority social work departments to fail to acknowledge any responsibilities on their part, a luxury denied England and Wales. Such an imbalance has also made it harder to make the shift towards community care within the NHS.

In offering an explanation for the lower profile of a community care strategy in Scotland, an official thought it stemmed from the fact that in England 'there has been a very definite central initiative which involved earmarked money and therefore community care has become almost a centrally funded programme'. In Scotland a policy of 'devolving responsibility and the finance to local agencies' is favoured. Moreover, 'we were never quite certain what we actually meant by community care and certainly we were quite clear that what was meant by different people was different'. The most recent circular on community care (Scottish Office 1985), in common with the 1977 English priorities statement, defines the term as embracing 'everything outside of institutions whether they are health or social work institutions, that this was part of a spectrum and that we weren't picking out one area to develop'. Boards are expected to be flexible in meeting individual needs which may involve community care *or* institutional care.

> The reason we've [that is, SHHD] put the emphasis on community care is because it's apparent that there is rather too much emphasis at present on institutional care but it's not a hobby horse and there is no special programme and that's why I think that we have not given it so much emphasis as they have in England.

A policy of maintaining a long-stay institutional sector is defended on the following grounds within the SHHD:

> We reckon it is better. This is an unfashionable view with the voluntary agencies, that there are people [the mentally handicapped and the elderly with mental disability] being looked after in hospital. It may not be the ideal place for them but they are being looked after . . .

The policy emphasis is said to be on preventing inappropriate admissions to long-stay institutions rather than on closing down institutions through a policy of discharge *in toto*.

> We need to rejig the service . . . but I do not accept this argument that appears to have gained currency after the Welsh initiative that we can close the mental handicap hospitals. You can't without recreating them in a form . . .

Merely describing how different Scotland is from England and, to an even greater extent, from Wales does not explain why this difference should remain so deep-seated. Why is the professional and service orientation so distinctive? Martin concludes his review of services for the mentally ill with the harsh judgement that in Scotland there has been 'an excess of complacency and a lack of self-examination both in the central department and in the relevant professions' (page 72). A 'lack of curiosity', as we pointed out in Chapter 1, may be part of the problem in developing new services and in innovating. Its origins may lie in national culture and experience, or it may reflect the relatively comfortable (and protected) resource position in which Scotland finds itself which induces a degree of complacency and a commitment to system maintenance. There is no incentive, or compulsion, to take stock of the limitations of institutional provision or to look afresh at the goals of services for the priority care groups. *SHAPE*, and other policy statements, may have sounded all the right notes but the lack of commitment and follow through is remarkable unless one appreciates that the professional and service context is so different from England and Wales and has been so for over a century.

Whether the priorities documents, and therefore national planning, have produced any results is uncertain although the evidence available suggests that in general they have not. As we reported earlier, a study by health economists at the University of Aberdeen has demonstrated that *SHAPE* priorities do not appear to be being met. Other evidence in relation to a particular priority area – psychogeriatric provision – confirms this conclusion (Hunter and others 1984).

Moreover, although no attempt was made by the SHHD to monitor the implementation of *The Way Ahead*, the Working Party on Health Priorities requested information on what health boards had spent on particular health programmes as an indication of how far there had been a shift in emphasis towards programmes accorded priority in the memorandum. Analyses were obtained for the four financial years, 1974/75 to 1977/78, according to which there had been an increase in the share of expenditure going to care of the elderly but no increase in the share going to mental illness or mental handicap services. Over the period a larger proportion of the growth monies in real terms went to the acute sector than to the combined programmes providing long term care.

On the other hand, according to Scottish Office officials, activity trends nationally *do* show that progress is in line with *SHAPE* priorities although they conceal marked differences between health boards. While conceding that progress has been very slow for a variety of reasons (some of which have been considered above), officials seem confident that the trends will continue in the desired direction and that a revised *SHAPE* will maintain the momentum if it is agreed that existing priorities should be retained. Nevertheless, as the former Minister for Health and Social Work, John MacKay, said at the 1986 centenary conference of the Psychiatric Nurses Association Scotland:

> I am aware of the great problem we have to treat your particular specialty plus the care of the elderly at the front of our priorities and I have a lot of sympathy for health boards and health board chairmen who actually have to battle day in day out on the ground to try to keep that priority up because, dare I say to you, that some of your colleagues in the acute sector have a far quicker route to the ear of the media and can, frankly, produce a much greater degree of public sympathy and public support, and it is very difficult for health boards, and indeed for ministers, to try to keep their eye on the three priority groups and not be deflected sometimes by the pressures that are on us to invest vast sums of money in some of the very clever, very high technology medicine . . . which is available.

Of course, similar pressures are brought to bear on Ministers in the English and Welsh departments.

c. *Wales*

In Wales, the community care initiative has been pursued in two ways which are intended to be complementary: first, there is an overall commitment to a community care strategy; and second, there is the All Wales Strategy for the Development of Services for Mentally Handicapped People. We consider the content of the Strategy in more detail in Chapter 5 as part of a case study of policies for the mentally handicapped in each of the three countries.

A circular issued in February 1983 (Welsh Office 1983b) announced the Secretary of State's decisions on the issues raised in the 1981 consultative document on *Care in the Community*. In addition to extensions to the system of joint finance, the circular adopted the suggestion that NHS funds should be earmarked within the Welsh Office for use on community care projects. In the first instance, earmarking would allow the development of community based services for the mentally handicapped.

Developments in community care in Wales are very different from those in England and, more especially, Scotland. The Welsh Office is committed at the highest political and official levels to recasting its services for the mentally handicapped upon the principle that such people have a right to normal patterns of life within the community. Its 'unequivocal commitment to a community based system of care' distinguishes it from England and, to an even greater extent, Scotland (Wistow 1985, page 77). The DHSS shied away from a similar strategy to the All Wales model when it was clear that the nursing profession was fiercely opposed to it. One for us has summarised the position in Britain as follows:

> ... this is not to say that the 'right' strategy has necessarily been adopted in Wales: but it possesses a greater degree of internal coherence and political support than has been evident in England – or Scotland, for that matter (Wistow 1985, page 78).

To some extent the All Wales Strategy has become synonymous with the Care in the Community initiative in Wales. It has certainly had the effect of overshadowing community care developments in other client groups although there is no evidence to suggest that this actually hindered progress. But there are differences between the two as an official explained:

> The Care in the Community programme is a sort of an *ad hoc* thing which people can pick up where they want to on particular projects. [The Mental Handicap Strategy] was meant to be a sort of blockbuster approach and to ensure that there would be no blocks along the way ... If we used the existing mechanisms it depended

upon the vote of a health authority to say 'right, we agree'. We didn't want a political bar in the middle.

Agreement on the ground among professionals could be jeopardised by health authority members refusing to agree. 'Ministers didn't want that.'

Unlike 'conventional' community care developments the Strategy is not dependent on health authorities agreeing to put resources into it.

The Secretary of State has got the direct power to put the money where he wants it. And it's a specific power [for Wales alone], it's not available to the Secretary of State for Social Services [in England] who didn't think he wanted it. And it's only available, at present, for mental handicap services because the Act of Parliament specifically requires the consent of the Treasury to the exercise of the power. There is nothing in principle to stop us applying for similar consent in relation to the elderly, or mental illness, or whatever.

Although it is not the intention exactly to mirror the Strategy in other sectors, the funding mechanism might be used in relation to other special initiatives, for example in care of the elderly. Officials accept that a possible price to pay for the 'blockbuster approach' with regard to mental handicap services has been a diversion of attention from other areas of community care. To this extent the Strategy does not fit 'terribly comfortably' into the broader Care in the Community programme. However, the available evidence is hard to interpret and complaints to the effect that it is all very well pumping resources into mental handicap services but what about those services which are being squeezed may be no more than, as one official put it, 'part of the old game of pressing government for more money'.

SUMMARY

Perhaps the central point to emerge from our review of community care policy is the quite different ways in which Scotland and Wales have departed from the policy position evident in England. On the one hand, in Scotland, a commitment to community care runs counter to the presence of powerful professional interests who perceive the problem and its solution differently and who favour 'more of the same'; on the other hand, in Wales, there is great political determination and commitment to make a reality of community care and no opposing interests (which do not, in any case, appear to be well organised) have been allowed to muddy the waters or act as a barrier to progress.

The different orientation to community care is a readily observable feature of the Scottish social care setting. We commented on the continuing adherence to an institutional sector with a stress on the need for maintaining large numbers of beds. This is the current reality but it continues to be a top priority for many professional groups. Whether the higher levels of provision, the general lack of pressure on services, the existence of a different administrative and professional outlook are singly or in some combination explanatory variables for this state of affairs is not possible to say on the basis of our evidence. Our suspicion is that some mix of these, and other features we have touched upon relating to the Scottish Office's origins, may be responsible. The same features, but displaying the opposite effect, namely, a genuine as distinct from symbolic commitment to community care, are evident in Wales.

It would seem, then, that in these different approaches to the general shared policy theme of community care marked differences in specific policy formulation and implementation exist within each of the three countries. It is not simply a means-ends distinction, however, because the interaction between means and ends is much more complex as we conclude in Chapter 8.

Despite the various differences in emphasis and meaning which we have noted here, the underlying assumption of community care policies across Britain has consistently been the need to shift the balance between health and social services reponsibilities towards the latter. Even the concept of care by the community implies an extended role for social services departments in stimulating, supporting and monitoring informal care. It follows, therefore, that two conditions must be achieved if community care is to become a reality: first, additional resources must be diverted into the personal social services; and second, the shift in the balance of responsibilities requires a degree of integrated planning at local level. The extent to which central departments have developed mechanisms which enable these conditions to be met is the subject of some considerable variation in each of the three countries as the foregoing description and analysis demonstrates. These divergencies are identified and discussed in the next chapter in our review of policies for mentally handicapped people and, more substantially, in Chapters 6 and 7.

Chapter 5
COMMUNITY CARE FOR MENTALLY HANDICAPPED
PEOPLE: A CASE STUDY IN POLICY DIVERSITY

INTRODUCTION

In this chapter the focus of our comparison switches from more generalised policies for community care to their consequences for a particular client group. Our aim is to map the ways in which the community care initiative has taken shape over the last decade and a half in the context of services for mentally handicapped people since limitations of space do not permit a review of developments for all the priority groups.

There are, however, sound reasons for selecting mental handicap as the area for more detailed study of the extent of progress to date. First, in all three countries during the early 1970s, it was the subject of the earliest national client group plans. Second, there is general agreement that the relatively small size and discrete nature of the client group make it the most manageable of the priority groups to plan for and resource. Lastly, and related to the previous point, experience of developments in this field is expected to pave the way for related developments in other priority groups.

DEVELOPING SERVICES FOR MENTALLY HANDICAPPED
PEOPLE

The fundamental element of policies for developing community care for mentally handicapped people is common to all three countries and, indeed, to each of the priority groups. The principal task has been seen as one of reducing hospital provision while building up residential, day and other support services in the community. However, differences rapidly emerge in two respects: first, the baseline levels of provision for mental handicap vary among the three countries, so that each has started from a different position; and second, there are divergencies between them in respect of the mix of services which they are ultimately aiming to achieve (Wistow 1985). In the 1970s these divergencies were particularly acute between Scotland, on the one hand, and England and Wales on the other. The DHSS and Welsh Office jointly published a White Paper, *Better Services for the Mentally Handicapped*, in 1971. This document laid down a set of basic

Table 6 Targets and achievements 1970/71 to 1980/81: Great Britain *

| | Places provided | Places required | | Shortfall/ overprovision | Increase/decrease in places | | Achieved as |
| | *1970/71* | *per 100,000* | *Total* | | *Required* | *Achieved 1980/81* | *% Target* † |
	nos	nos	nos	%	nos	nos	%
					Hospital beds (all ages)		
England	59,000	68	31,500	47	−27,500	−10,400	38
Scotland	7,700	120	6,300	18	−1,400	−1,100	79
Wales	2,700	68	1,900	30	−800	−250	31
					Local authority homes and hostels (all ages)		
England	4,785	70	32,400**	577	+27,615	+7,927	29
Scotland	59	43	2,200**	3,629	+2,141	+689	32
Wales	228	70	1,900**	733	+1,672	+447	27
					Day care (adults)		
England	21,892	150	69,400	217	+47,508	+21,735	46
Scotland	2,863	150	7,800	172	+4,937	+2,022	41
Wales	965	150	4,100	325	+3,135	+1,801	58

* Data for health services are at 31 December in the relevant financial year and data for social services are at 31 March in the same financial year.

** The target for homes and hostels in England and Wales specifically encompassed voluntary and private provision as well as local authority services. In Scotland, however, both the target and the shortfall were defined solely in terms of local authority provision.

† The targets were to be achieved over a twenty year period in England and Wales but over one of 'about ten years' in Scotland.

Sources: DHSS, Health and Personal Social Services Statistics; Welsh Office, Health and Personal Social Services Statistics for Wales; Scottish Office, Scottish Health Statistics and SWSG Statistical Bulletin.

principles to underpin the development in England and Wales of a more locally based 'modern' service (DHSS and Welsh Office 1971). In addition, targets were set for reductions in the level of hospital provision and for increases in local authority residential and day care services (Table 6). It was intended that these targets should be achieved over a twenty year period. The reduction in hospital populations was initially to be achieved by the prevention of inappropriate admissions and, subsequently, by discharging patients with no continuing need of inpatient medical or nursing services. The transition to the new service model was to be achieved within a framework of effective joint planning between health and local authorities. In the interim, however, an investment programme was launched to bring existing hospitals up to acceptable minimum standards.

Much preparatory work on the White Paper was accomplished before responsibility for personal social services was devolved from the DHSS to the Welsh Office, though the document's immediate origins lay in the enquiry into conditions at Ely Hospital in Cardiff. The White Paper provided a common framework for development for the next decade or so. However, the preparation of an *All Wales Strategy for Mentally Handicapped People* (Welsh Office 1983a) marked the emergence of a clear divergence between England and Wales in terms both of service objectives and also of mechanisms for transferring responsibility from health to social services. By contrast there has been little movement on policy within Scotland and the situation there remains out of step with that in either England or Wales. We begin our case study with Scotland.

a. *Scotland*

The production by the Scottish Office of its own strategy for mental handicap – the 'Blue Book' of 1972 – showed that the objectives of the English and Welsh 1971 White Paper were, in broad terms, also shared in Scotland (SHHD and SED 1972). However, while this memorandum restated the principles and objectives of the White Paper, it also contained a number of different emphases. For example, the Scottish Office targets were to be achieved within a ten year period, half the time allowed by the DHSS and the Welsh Office. More fundamentally, there was an important difference between the scale of the shift towards community care being planned for in Scotland compared with that in England and Wales (see Table 6). This difference in approach was expressed in two different ways. First, the 'Blue Book' envisaged that the proportion of the client group to be accommodated in some form of residential setting (that is,

101

hospital and local authority residential services combined) would be some 20 per cent greater than in England and Wales. Second, the planned number of hospital beds was to be almost three-quarters of that combined total, whereas a roughly equal number of places in hospital and residential homes was being planned for by the DHSS and the Welsh Office. In other words, hospitals were to provide inpatient care for almost twice as large a proportion of the client group in Scotland as in the remainder of Britain. As a result of these differences in the planning targets and in the historical service baselines, the required reduction in hospital bed numbers in Scotland was considerably less than that in England and Wales. Yet, at the same time, a more substantial increase in local authority residential places remained necessary in Scotland because this form of provision was all but non-existent there in the early 1970s.

The hospital and institutional emphasis of policy in Scotland was further underlined in 1979 when the Scottish Office published its revised strategy, *A Better Life* (SHHD and SED 1979). This document argued that an even higher level of hospital and residential care provision was needed and the target was increased from 160 to 180 places per 100,000 population. In fact, the document considered that 200 places per 100,000 would be the more proper estimate of need. However, in view of the low levels of existing provision, this was not considered a realistic policy objective. The target for England and Wales was, by contrast, only 138 places per 100,000 population. Thus policy in Scotland has consistently placed more weight on hospital services than in England and Wales and this remains the Scottish Office preference. We quoted in Chapter 4 the Scottish Office official who believed that it was preferable for certain vulnerable groups of people to be looked after in hospital even if this was not the ideal environment for them. The same official went on to explain that while community care was receiving some emphasis to counter-balance the institutional bias 'it's not a hobby horse and there is no special programme and that's why I think we have not given it so much emphasis as they have in England'. The emphasis is very much on making sure everyone is looked after and if this means a hospital bed then it is preferable to being left without shelter. This notion of the hospital serving as a refuge or sanctuary emerged in the view of one official: while ultimately 'ensuring that everyone is in the right place . . . at the moment let's make sure that people have still got a roof over their heads'. It is a view which the programme planning group (PPG) on services for the mentally handicapped in Scotland expressed in its 1979 report where it argued that 'many severely mentally handicapped persons *are in need of protection* from the community: the *protective secure life of the hospital* represents for them a suitable pattern of care' (SHHD and SED 1979, paragraph 7.24, page 74, emphasis added). It continues: 'many mentally handicapped people may be more lonely and more restricted in an uncaring community than in the arguably artificial but at least richer social life enjoyed in hospital'. Moreover, the PPG does not envisage 'any meaningful transfer of existing patients' from hospital to residential care because of the shortfall in provision and the emphasis on avoiding admission to hospital. In addition to these pragmatic grounds, it was also acknowledged that the most influential of professional opinion (on the health side) also favoured the retention of a substantial number of hospital beds.

Further evidence of the distinctive policy stance and service mix in Scotland is provided in a first report from the Scottish Health Service Information Service Division on the study of the balance of care for mentally handicapped adults in Scotland carried out between July 1983 and August 1985 (Baker and Urquhart 1986). The authors state that between 1974 and 1983 the number of adults resident in mental handicap hospitals reduced only marginally during the period, mainly because of a continuing demand for hospital places. The study found that the majority of the hospital resident population were not very highly dependent or inclined to very difficult behaviour. 'Hospitals were housing a clear majority of virtually all groups of people in fully-staffed residential circumstances – even 58 per cent of the group defined as 'relatively able and apparently problem-free' (paragraph 20, page 79). It is possible that the imbalance is a reflection of the continuing under-supply of alternative places, particularly when those individuals entering hospital appear to be able and apparently problem-free and, in the opinion of the researchers, eminently eligible for a placement elsewhere. However, establishing cause and effect is not easy. The researchers conclude by arguing that from the results of the study it appears that 'all but a few per cent of the people currently resident in hospital would be *capable* of living in fully-staffed accommodation outwith hospital . . . [but that] only a small minority of hospital staff would seem at present to endorse [this] statement' (paragraph 7.2, page 86). Given the views expressed by the PPG in its 1979 report, mentioned above, it is not only hospital staff who appear wedded to a hospital solution for many mentally handicapped people.

Scarcely surprising, therefore, that there has been little movement since the late 1970s in the development and review of policy within Scotland and that the overall culture continues to be one which places greater emphasis on institutional solutions generally and on the contribution of hospitals in particular than is to be found in either England or Wales. In June 1986, addressing the centenary conference of the Psychiatric Nursing Association Scotland, the former Minister for Health and Social Work, John MacKay, reaffirmed his commitment to such a policy. He said:

> ... occasionally I am under some attack from some of the pressure groups in this field because I will not say that I think care in the community should be the be all and end all and I do say quite frequently to them that I believe a mix is required and that hospitals will and will always have an important part to play in the care of the mentally handicapped.

The Minister went on to say how he attached great importance to the replacement of old hospital buildings with new or upgraded facilities. This had to be done in tandem with building up community care services. 'I'm not one of those people who thinks it's an either or, I think it has to be both.' If hospitals are seen as inappropriate places for the mentally handicapped it is to *prevent admissions* rather than *transferring patients* to community care and is in marked contrast to developments elsewhere in Britain, notably England. *SHAPE* expresses the difference in approach succinctly:

> ... a major constraint on any massive reduction in the number of existing hospital residents is that the majority, many of whom are elderly, have been in hospital for a very long time and would find it difficult to adapt to life outside. There is more scope for preventing long lengths of stay for new admissions by increasing support for the mentally handicapped and their families in the community (SHHD 1980b, paragraph II.72, page 35).

SHAPE therefore recommends that a shift of emphasis from hospital to community care should proceed on the basis of preventing inappropriate admissions to hospital.

b. England

In England, a review of the White Paper's strategy was published by the DHSS in 1980 in which the original planning targets were reaffirmed (DHSS 1980). By this time, however, the balance and model of care which they implied was under challenge. A growing lobby, reflecting in part the influence of the Jay committee (Parliament 1979), was questioning the need for specialist hospital provision on the grounds that mental handicap was a long term disability rather than an illness susceptible to cure. The House of Commons Social Services Committee's (1985) report on community care went a long way towards endorsing this view, arguing that all but a minority of mentally handicapped people could be accommodated within domestic housing with support services being provided according to their individual needs. The report also favoured the transfer of mental handicap services to local government at the end of a ten year period. In practice, however, the NHS is continuing to develop its own residential services, often in purpose-built units and sometimes on, or adjacent to, hospital sites. The underlying assumption is that they will be targeted on the most dependent of the present hospital residents, but some health authorities seem to be providing for a wide range of dependency levels, in some cases because local authorities are unable or unwilling to make such provision.

The principal development to emerge from the DHSS since the 1980 policy review is the Care in the Community initiative. As we noted earlier, its overwhelming focus is on reducing hospital populations through patient transfers rather than the more gradualist one of preventing further hospital admissions. At the same time, the Department has argued that the initiative should be implemented within existing resources on the assumption that, with the addition of short-term bridging funds to cover the period of transition, the new pattern of services will be no more expensive than the present hospital ones. What this leaves out of account are the widely acknowledged inadequacies of resources in many existing hospitals and also the need to meet the demand for services from mentally handicapped people who have never entered the hospital system and who will not directly benefit from the resources transferred from hospital with their former residents. There is also some evidence that resources transferred from long-stay hospitals are as likely to remain in the health service as to be transferred into the local government sector (Wistow and Hardy 1986). Consequently, the local authority role in providing locally based services may be less substantial than DHSS policies have traditionally anticipated. Yet this shift towards a focus on patient transfers has taken place at a time when the volume of need outside the hospital sector is also increasing. The number of parents keeping their mentally handicapped children at home has grown over the last ten to 15 years. As a result, not only has the demand for respite care and family support services grown, but also the number of mentally handicapped people living with elderly carers. In other words, the very success of community care policies in the past has stored up demands for community services to which DHSS policies seem ill-equipped to respond.

c. *Wales*

By contrast, the approach in Wales differs considerably. Firstly, and most substantially, the starting point in Wales has been to re-examine the model of care contained in the 1971 White Paper in the light of changed understanding of the needs, problems and potential of mentally handicapped people. As the Welsh Secretary noted at the public launch of the policy review:

> . . . there is now indisputable evidence . . . that not only can some of even the most profoundly mentally handicapped be maintained at home by the family, if the right services are available; but that, given the right pattern of support, a large number – possibly the majority – of mentally handicapped people can take their place very successfully as active and accepted members of their communities.

The All Wales Strategy (Welsh Office 1983a) fully reflected this background with its emphasis on the rights of mentally handicapped people 'to normal patterns of life within the community' (paragraph 2.1, page i,1). Thus it was argued that they should have access to accommodation in ordinary housing and support services appropriate to their own needs New 'purpose-built hostels, hospitals or units should not form part of the new patterns' (paragraph 4.2, page v, 6). The tenets of the normalisation philosophy have found strong echoes in the Welsh Strategy, therefore.

The second element of the Welsh Office's approach flows from this model of care. Responsibility for coordinating the development of local plans has been placed in the hands of the bodies to whom will fall the major responsibility for overseeing the delivery of comprehensive local services in accordance with the Strategy: the social services departments of the eight Welsh counties. Third, substantial new resources will be made available by the Welsh Office to the counties in an investment programme which builds up over ten years. Apart from the contrast with the 'cost-neutral' assumption in England, the availability of new monies gives the Welsh Office leverage to ensure the compatibility of local plans with the national strategy. It has already turned down a number of county plans and, in one case at least, this is said to have produced a 'road to Damascus conversion'. The Strategy is not, however, intended to be a rigid blueprint that is slavishly followed by field authorities. Rather it is, in the words of one official, 'about a cumulative build-up of investment which accelerates in the second five years when we've got more confidence about where we are going'. To this end, two 'vanguard areas' have been identified as sites for the most rapid and complete establishment of model services. At the same time, monitoring is seen as a key element in the implementation of the Strategy. At national level an All Wales Advisory Panel on the development of mental handicap services was established in late 1983. One of its tasks is to advise on the monitoring and evaluation of the Strategy and to advise the Welsh Office on

106

whether it appears to be meeting its principal aims and objectives. Locally, the onus for monitoring its implementation falls on the counties and guidance on this task has already been issued (Welsh Office 1985a).

The final element of the All Wales Strategy is its emphasis on building up services in the community to prevent hospital admissions. Bed reductions and closures will gradually emerge from this process but there is no equivalent to the ministerial push for patient transfers which has been so marked in England. On the contrary, the ministerial emphasis has been on the prevention of inappropriate admissions and hence more akin to the approach favoured in Scotland. The Secretary of State has acknowledged that the 'inadequacy of care in the community creates a cycle of dependence on institutional care because this is often the only option open to families who can no longer cope on their own' (Welsh Office 1983a, page i). The All Wales Strategy is, therefore, explicitly an attempt to break into that cycle and, in effect, to create an environment in which the need for large-scale hospital services gradually withers away as comprehensive alternative services become established within local communities.

The story of how this radical and principled approach to the promotion of community care for mentally handicapped people came to be launched has yet to be fully told. The factors behind it were undoubtedly 'many and diverse' as one official acknowledged. Apart from a recognition of a general service imbalance, the Ely hospital scandal in Wales in 1969 proved seminal. However, the initial proposals for service development, circulated in confidence to Welsh health authorities in 1980/81, were based on an entirely different model of care. Prepared within the Department and with a substantial medical input, the plan was to build 49 32-bed units on hospital sites and to increase the number of consultant psychiatrists. Unilateral planning by health authorities, with no immediate consultation with local authorities, was also proposed. Unfavourable contrasts were made with England about what was seen as Wales' 'backward step' (*Arcade* 1981). The resulting political interest and controversy led the Secretary of State to give top priority to the creation of a comprehensive strategy which would comprise a genuinely community based service. Also apparently influential was the belief that mental handicap was the most straightforward of the priority groups to tackle and that success here would give people the confidence to start investing in similar strategies for other groups. Finally, and possibly most important, the political will was there, although it is not clear exactly why. Whatever the reasons, the Secretary of State, according to one official who helped draw up the Strategy:

107

... really did put his back into this ... Without that willingness to push the thing through we wouldn't have got anywhere no matter how much people had put into it at official level or out there in the field.

The end result has been a coherent strategy for the development of locally based services, backed up by relatively substantial earmarked resources. In both these respects, Wales appears to have significant advantages over much of England and Scotland. Nonetheless, much remains to be accomplished before service users can experience the potential benefits of the strategy to the full. A great deal is being expected of local officials in a context where inter-agency planning has been under-developed (see below) but expectations have been raised by the high profile accorded to the strategy. Not surprisingly, therefore, as the implementation phase has got underway, problems have begun to emerge in planning and programming new developments, while some consumers have criticised the apparently slow pace of investment in practical services (Beyer and others 1986). Given that so much new ground is being broken in terms of both substantive policy and administrative processes, the strategy's implementation is likely to be problematic if not patchy. Such teething problems should not, however, be allowed to obscure the essentially coherent and fundamental nature of the Welsh Office's initiative, especially as compared with its governmental counterparts elsewhere in the country.

SUMMARY

By the early 1980s, therefore, three rather different approaches to community care for mentally handicapped people could be discerned in the constituent parts of Great Britain. Differences existed in the preferred balance of health and local authority responsibilities and in the basic beliefs about the needs and potentialities of individuals within the client group. Underlying these differences were the differing strengths of various interests within and outside the government machine in each of the three countries.

In Scotland, a medical view of mental handicap held sway basing its strength on the traditional large institutions and on the health dominated policy planning groups from which voluntary agencies and consumer interests were largely excluded. In England, where health and social services policy has a more corporate base, the policy outcome was a more even handed compromise between health and social service interests. As a DHSS official associated with the preparation of the 1971 White Paper subsequently acknowledged, its contents gave some satisfaction to most of the participants in the 'hospital/no hospital debate' (Donges 1982). In Wales, where the policy process was both more open and broadly based with a significant input from voluntary groups and where the medical interests were small in number, the output was different again: in effect, Wales is the only part of the United Kingdom to adopt as official policy the notion that mental handicap is not an illness.

The correlation between how broadly based the policy process was, the relative strengths of social services and consumer interests, and the ultimate policy output is undeniably strong. Much less easy to explain is the basis of the differential degree of power apparently exercised by the same interests in England, Wales and Scotland, although we speculated on this in the final part of Chapter 4. It is an issue which would repay closer comparative study – as would the outputs of services on the ground. One of us has previously noted that, since 'the various health departments in Great Britain now seem set on rather different courses with regard to the balance between hospital and other provision, a clear opportunity exists to compare systematically services operating with different mixes of hospital, hostel and housing provision' (Wistow 1985, page 78). It remains to be seen, however, whether there is sufficient commitment on the part of policy-makers to take advantage of such opportunities or whether policies will continue to be determined by the individual and relatively isolated constellations of beliefs and interests that surround the health departments in London, Edinburgh and Cardiff.

Collaboration, or joint working, is a cornerstone of the community care initiative as both this and the last chapter have demonstrated. It is a highly contentious subject and the record of quite different agencies working together united in a common purpose is extremely variable. Variation is a feature *within* each of the countries but is, if anything, more marked *between* them. While the national dimension was the focus of this and the previous three chapters, the local dimension is the subject of the next two chapters in which we review the collaborative machinery and joint planning mechanisms that have been spawned across Britain.

INTRODUCTION

Central government policies for community care imply inter-service collaboration locally, no less than nationally. Indeed, a fundamental aim of the DHSS, the Welsh Office and – to a lesser extent – the Scottish Office has been to create patterns of 'local-local relations' (Wistow 1982) or 'periphery-periphery relations' (Hunter 1983a), which promote the extension of community care. In essence, the approach has been one of seeking to recreate at local level, by means of collaborative planning between health and local authorities, the boundary spanning perspectives of the national health departments (Webb and Wistow 1985). The essential elements of various initiatives by central government have included: boundary coterminosity; a legal mandate; machinery for joint planning; and financial incentives for collaboration. In this chapter we concentrate on structural issues and reserve, until Chapter 7, discussion of financial mechanisms designed to promote inter-agency planning for community care at local level.

ARRANGEMENTS FOR COLLABORATION: ENGLAND

Health and local authority structures

The present structures for the local administration of health and related services date from the simultaneous reorganisations of the NHS and local government which came into effect in 1974. Although modified on the health side by the 1982 restructuring of the NHS, the abolition of the Greater London Council and Metropolitan Counties in 1986 had few implications for local government's relationship with the health service. The need to promote inter-service cooperation was a central theme in the build up to the 1974 reorganisations (Wistow 1982). Its most obvious expression was the principle of one-to-one coterminosity: the drawing of common boundaries for area health authorities and those local authorities responsible for personal social services.

The value of one-to-one coterminosity has remained a controversial matter. A study for the Royal Commission on the NHS (1979, paragraph 7.4, page 50) found that 'a surprisingly large number of respondents expressed the view that the principle of coterminosity was irrelevant or worse . . .' Some respondents felt it had led to the creation of health authority boundaries inappropriate to the operation of the NHS since the catchment areas of local authority and health services were not the same. However, a closer review of the evidence produced the intriguing result that support for coterminosity was strongest among those working in community services and that those furthest away from such services supported it least. Certainly the proposal to abolish coterminosity as the basic building block of the NHS structure under the *Patients First* proposals (DHSS and Welsh Office 1979) attracted considerable criticism from local authority interests and also those working at area level in the health service. By early 1982 a national survey suggested that opinion within the NHS was coalescing around the view that coterminosity had been valuable in getting collaboration underway but that its loss would not, on the whole, be a permanent setback: 73 per cent of respondents indicated that coterminosity had been 'an essential precondition for the growth of collaboration' in their area but only 36 per cent considered its loss would 'undermine attempts to develop collaboration for the foreseeable future' (Wistow and Fuller 1983, page 29). We record below the apparent consequences of the subsequent boundary changes for the formal arrangements for collaboration.

Boundary coterminosity was backed up by two further statutory requirements. First, health and local authorities were placed under a legal obligation to cooperate with each other, in order 'to secure and advance the health and welfare of the population'. Second, they were required to establish joint consultative committees (JCCs) to advise them on the performance of such duties and also on the planning and operation of services of common concern. While these joint committees were to be advisory rather than executive bodies, the DHSS hoped that the importance of effective collaboration would be reflected in the appointment to them of senior members from each authority (DHSS 1974). Cooperation at member level was also built into the membership of the new health authorities, four of whose 15 or more members were nominated by the corresponding local authorities.

Joint planning

The emphasis on building structures to facilitate inter-authority cooperation was rapidly followed by detailed guidance on joint planning. Health and local authorities were urged by the DHSS to develop genuinely integrated planning processes in which 'each authority contributes to all stages of the other's planning from the first step in developing common policies and strategies to the production of operational plans to carry them out' (DHSS 1976a). The primary mechanisms for carrying out this process were multidisciplinary planning teams: a Joint Care Planning Team (JCPT) of senior officers drawn from each matching health and local authority supported, where appropriate, by sub teams with responsibility for particular client groups or issues of mutual interest (for example, social work support to the health service). The joint planning initiative was intimately bound up with the establishment of an NHS planning system, also introduced in 1976, and with which it shared a number of common objectives (Wistow 1982). These included, most fundamentally, the provision of a means for adjusting the balance of resources within the NHS and between it and other agencies. Thus the guidance stressed that 'effective joint planning is vital to the Government's overall strategy of developing community-based services to the fullest extent practicable so that people are kept out of hospitals and other institutions and supported within the community' (DHSS 1976a).

An earmarked financial allocation – joint finance – was introduced at the same time to provide an immediately tangible purpose for the joint planning machinery (see Chapter 7). After this initial flurry of activity, however, local agencies were effectively left to operationalise – or not – their own approaches to joint planning. As with the NHS planning system, local experience was not systematically or comprehensively monitored. Nor was such evidence as did emerge about progress in joint planning followed up with individual authorities. Indeed, the next major initiative taken by the centre was one which the DHSS (1981b), no less than local practitioners and external observers (Wistow and Webb 1980; Outer Circle Policy Unit 1980), ultimately accepted would make local collaborative planning more difficult to achieve. This development arose from the proposal of the incoming Conservative administration to abolish area health authorities (AHAs), the tier of NHS administration coterminous with local social services authorities (DHSS and Welsh Office 1979). In the event, some of the potentially more disruptive consequences of these proposals were reduced by the replacement of one-to-one coterminosity by 'whole number coterminosity', under which the boundaries of more than one health authority were wholly contained within those of a single local social services authority.

In addition, one-to-one coterminosity was retained for two-fifths (42 per cent) of such local authorities, largely those in which a single district AHA had previously operated (Wistow and Fuller 1986). Nonetheless, boundary overlaps were a significant feature of the new structural arrangements: one third (35 per cent) of social services

112

authorities related to health authorities which also occupied territory within the boundaries of a neighbouring social services department. In all, 45 per cent related to more than one health authority. From 1982, therefore, one-to-one coterminosity – the basic building block of the enabling structures introduced only eight years previously – no longer existed in most (54 per cent) localities. By this time, and paradoxically, the DHSS was placing renewed emphasis on the need for joint planning to implement its Care in the Community strategy (DHSS 1981b; 1983b). A basic question raised by this apparent inconsistency on the part of the DHSS was whether it would make any real difference. Had collaborative planning become so firmly a part of NHS and local government procedures that it would be able to withstand the disruptions of structural upheaval; or had so little been achieved that a rearrangement of structures would be of minimal consequence?

The record of joint planning

Up to restructuring in 1982, local joint planning was marked by two features: the establishment of substantial amounts of formal planning machinery, and widespread agreement that such machinery had failed to deliver the goods. Genuine joint planning of the kind outlined by the DHSS in 1976 was scarcely even a gleam in the eyes of local planners. Based on unrealistic and over-optimistic assumptions about the possibility of developing comprehensive rational planning processes across agency boundaries (Webb and Wistow 1985) achievements were modest (Booth 1981; Glennerster and others 1983; Wistow and Fuller 1983). JCCs tended to be talking shops and JCPTs preoccupied with joint finance and other issues which fell well short of strategic client group planning. Generally speaking – but by no means universally – inter-authority communications improved and personal relationships were cordial. However, improved relationships should not be equated with effective joint planning. For the most part, local experiences at best amounted to a form of 'parallel planning' based on consultation and information exchange (Jasp Team 1984; Wistow 1987).

An analysis of joint planning in seven contrasting localities over the three years from 1979 provided more data on its achievements (Jasp Team 1984). Distinguishing between three categories of output, the study found only two examples of joint plans for elderly people and children under five but 40 joint projects and 24 joint 'professional practices'. Most of these projects were, however, joint in name only, being social services schemes processed through the joint planning machinery purely for the purposes of securing joint finance. In contrast the 'professional practices' (such as multidisciplinary assessment procedures) were more genuinely joint in origin. They also more frequently originated from practitioners and operational managers rather than planning staff working through the formal planning machinery. As Norton and Rogers (1981, pages 136–137) also concluded, a bottom up, entrepreneurial approach to collaborative planning can often appear to pay bigger dividends than some formal planning procedures. However, the Jasp Team (1984) also emphasised the limits of this approach in achieving change on a client group or locality wide basis.

Nonetheless, the majority of authorities have been conscientious in following DHSS guidance to establish planning machinery, as national surveys have demonstrated (Wistow and Fuller 1983; 1986). Almost all authorities had JCPTs in 1982 whereas only two-thirds had an equivalent team of chief or senior officers in 1976. The number of officer sub-groups more than doubled over the same period and, more importantly, a significant shift took place in their subject matter: in 1982 most were concerned with services for the DHSS priority groups whereas, six years previously, there had been scarcely any joint planning machinery for these client groups. Considerable gaps remained, however: for example, less than half the localities had sub-groups for mental illness or physical handicap (Wistow and Fuller 1983). Thus, if less was achieved than the DHSS had initially hoped, health and local authorities nonetheless gave considerably greater attention to joint planning in the period after 1974. On an optimistic assessment, at least some of the basic preconditions for local joint planning were being established in England between 1976 and 1982 (Wistow and Fuller 1983) though Glennerster and others' (1983) more sceptical view that the DHSS had merely made it more difficult not to attempt to plan for the priority groups was clearly justified in some localities at least.

Whatever the case, a survey conducted in 1984 suggested that the pattern of joint planning machinery two years after restructuring was broadly similar to that reported two years previously. There had been some delays in re-establishing formal collaboration machinery but restructuring appeared to have created only a hiatus in joint planning (Wistow and Fuller 1986). Yet, these findings merely indicated that the gaps in the formal machinery had become no more marked (page 34), scarcely grounds for complacency in the context of experience up to 1982. In addition, the minority of localities which retained one-to-one coterminosity were found – generally speaking – to possess more fully developed arrangements for collaboration than those subjected to boundary change. Whether the new NHS structures have created new and permanent barriers to local joint planning for authorities in the latter group is, however, something which will emerge only over a longer period and in association with the impact of other influences such as resource scarcity and the post-Griffiths management processes. Indeed, the cumulative experience of research in this field is that enabling structures are only one among many factors which influence local joint planning. No less important influences include differences in financial resources, service stocks, professional viewpoints and personalities (Wistow and Fuller 1986).

'Progress in partnership'

In 1984 a joint working party was established by the DHSS together with the health and local authority associations to review arrangements for joint planning and joint finance. As its report, *Progress in Partnership* noted, 'behind the proposal (to establish the review) was a widespread sense of frustration that more had not been achieved through joint planning' (Working Group on Joint Planning 1985, paragraph 1.2, page 1). In keeping with the current climate in public sector management, the report stressed the importance of identifying specific tasks, placing responsibility for fulfilling them on named individuals and strengthening lines of accountability. Recognising that in the past too much had depended on 'the enthusiasm of individuals', the report saw strengthened JCCs as an 'engine to drive joint planning' (page i): senior councillors and health authority members were to join JCCs and play an active part in motivating officers; the focus of joint planning was to be 'total resource planning' rather than changes at the margin; annual reports on the work of JCCs should be submitted to the Secretary of State; and their meetings were to be opened to the public. The key step to making a reality of collaborative planning was seen as 'the establishment of small, genuinely joint planning teams for each group where services need developing, with balanced representation and close links with professional, voluntary and client interests, and the abandonment of single agency planning for the client groups' (page ii). Furthermore, the NHS general managers and local authority chief executives were recommended to 'ensure that there are nominated officers accountable for joint planning activities' (page ii).

The report was welcomed by the health and local authority associations and accepted by ministers. At the time of writing, a draft circular based on its recommendations is out for consultation (DHSS 1986). Perhaps predictably, there have been some local government reservations about the dangers of apparently becoming tied into review and accountability processes originating in and more properly belonging to the NHS (Murray 1986; Smart 1986). Over the next year

115

or two, however, health and local authorities are clearly going to be required to make a fresh and more positive start to joint planning. A more clearly defined framework is being laid down and, perhaps most importantly, failure is going to be more public. At the end of the day, however, the report itself recognised that 'progress in partnership' could not be guaranteed by the approach recommended: 'where genuine joint planning turns out not to be achieveable, it may have to be accepted that one of the authorities concerned should take lead responsibility for developing services for a particular group if there is otherwise no prospect of the required range of services being provided' (page i). For the present, however, we await the sounds of the new 'engine of joint planning' being kick-started into life.

ARRANGEMENTS FOR COLLABORATION: SCOTLAND

Health and local authority structures

As elsewhere in Britain existing arrangements for inter-agency collaboration stem from the 1974 reorganisation of the NHS. A key theme of the reforms was integration, and although this referred principally to closer working relationships between the three sectors comprising the NHS – primary care, community health, and hospitals – it also covered relations with local authorities which had hitherto been virtually ignored except in those fields where local government directly discharged health responsibilities. Following the 1974 reorganisation a proportion of places (about a quarter) on health boards are occupied by local authority representatives.

Despite a steady commitment to joint planning and collaboration displayed by the government across Britain, Scotland has been less obviously committed to this endeavour and the mechanisms and procedures introduced (and not introduced) over the past decade or so reflect this difference.

Since 1974 the boundaries of 11 out of the 15 health boards have matched those of regional (or island) authorities which are responsible for social work services. In Strathclyde Region, which covers about half the country's population, there are four health boards and this has produced particular problems (especially for the health boards) with regard to collaboration.

Until the second NHS restructuring in 1984, ten health boards had districts whose boundaries matched the lower tier local authorities, which were responsible, *inter alia*, for housing, in only a handful of cases. Since 1984 all health boards have established units of management (in place of districts in those boards which had them) following a protracted debate about whether or not boards should be permitted to decide for themselves whether to abolish districts or retain them (Hunter 1984). The debate resembled that conducted in Wales (see below) where areas were retained and districts abolished.

In Scotland it was argued that health boards should be abolished, since they were the equivalent of the area tier in England which disappeared in 1982, and that districts should become full health authorities rather than simply a management tier. However, because abolition of area health boards would have entailed a considerable upheaval and because the areas had, in the government's view, worked well since 1974 it was decided to leave them intact. Nevertheless concern over the size of health boards compared with English DHAs remained. Most DHAs cover populations of about 200,000 with large authorities, 500,000 and over, as the exception. Greater Glasgow Health Board covers a population of over one million and Lothian Health Board a population of three-quarters of a million. Only 6 per cent of DHAs have populations over 400,000 compared with 50 per cent of health boards; 70 per cent of DHAs fall within the population band 100,000 to 300,000. On the basis of these figures it was thought that the *districts* or, in some cases, amalgamations of districts should be retained in preference to areas. No doubt fears that an increase in the number of health authorities would bring forth calls for a regional tier which would lead to a re-emergence of the pre-1974 two tier structure of regional boards and boards of management also lay behind the decision to axe districts. However, the 1982/84 restructuring of the NHS across Britain led to the creation of greater structural differences at local level between England and Scotland (and Wales) than had existed at any time since 1948.

The original intention was that those boards which wished to retain their districts could do so if they put forward convincing arguments. Although such a strategy was in keeping with the SHHD's 'hands off' approach to managing the Scottish health service it proved unworkable and all ten boards with districts were instructed to abolish them (SHHD 1983).

Many of the units have the same boundaries as the districts they replaced. Others are subdivisions of former districts. Therefore, the position with regard to coterminosity between units and lower tier local authorities remains mixed. However, the important intermediate level for the purpose of joint planning is that of the health boards and regional councils and this remains unaffected by the 1984 changes. Therefore, the structural position in Scotland closely resembles that in Wales but differs significantly from that in England (see above).

Within Scotland the existence of coterminosity is believed to be important; certainly it is the view of the Minister for Health and Social Work that 'there's better cooperation' where health and local au-

117

thorities share common boundaries. Another factor, and possibly a more important one, alleged to aid collaboration is the scale of operations. As an SHHD official put it:

> . . . a factor one always has to bear in mind in Scotland is that it's a small place and people have more hats than they usually do in England and therefore it's easier for cooperation, you are more likely to come across people.

Despite such advantages, there is mounting evidence that joint planning and collaboration has not taken root in Scotland or been pursued with the same apparent vigour as in either England (or in parts of it at least) or Wales. We consider the reasons for this later although, as we concluded in Chapter 2, the structural position of the relevant Scottish Office departments is very different from their English and Welsh counterparts and seems likely to be a contributing factor.

There are two principal mechanisms for promoting collaboration between health and local authorities: joint liaison committees (JLCs) and their associated officer groups, and support finance. The remainder of this section is devoted to JLCs and their contribution to joint planning. Support finance is considered in the next chapter. Mention also needs to be made of health boards' own sporadic and uneven attempts at planning which have a 'joint' dimension since they include input from agencies other than health. There exists no formal local planning machinery akin to HCPTs or JCPTs in England but programme planning committees (PPCs) were set up by most health boards for a time following the 1974 reorganisation. Several boards have recently revived these committees, or have established similar groups, partly in response to criticism that the reports produced in the late 1970s do not appear to have been implemented, and partly in response to the requirement set out in the most recent circular on joint planning (Scottish Office 1985) that health boards and local authorities should produce ten year joint plans.

As we pointed out in Chapter 4, a feature of health service planning in Scotland is the absence of any rigid procedural approach. Accordingly, one local health planner has commented that 'the range of disparate arrangements made for planning in the management structure of Scottish health boards is a reflection of the varying needs for planning and the somewhat *laissez faire* attitude towards planning adopted by the central department' (Leary 1983, page 280).

Joint planning

In 1977 a working party on relationships between health boards and local authorities (SHHD 1977) reported and has guided all subsequent developments in this area. Its main recommendation was for the establishment of JLCs which would advise on the planning and operation of services of common concern. While JLCs represented the formal machinery the report also recommended close working arrangements between officers of health boards and local authorities. These would be more informal and would be concerned with ensuring proper coordination in day-to-day operations and in forward planning. The working party thought that there should be only one JLC in each region to deal with services at both regional and district levels. Arrangements in Strathclyde would be different since the region covers the area of four health boards.

The working party did not recommend that JLCs should be empowered to commit the constituent authorities since this would amount to an unacceptable erosion of responsibility from these authorities. JLCs were to be member and officer bodies and should meet at least three times a year. Working groups of officers were to be established to advise JLCs on particular issues of joint concern like care of the elderly, the mentally handicapped and so on.

JLCs are not statutory bodies and not all boards possess them although the majority does. Nonetheless, as one SHHD official observed, 'joint planning is no less effective in those boards because they don't have a JLC'. Indeed in some boards with JLCs, their value is questioned by SHHD officials. Apparently, making JLCs a statutory requirement was considered. 'We concluded that there was no point because there was no suggestion that they would ever be executive bodies.' The same official claimed that the English counterparts – JCCs – were statutory bodies for two reasons: first, they were introduced at the time of the 1974 NHS reorganisation, and when there is legislation it is customary 'to tip everything into it'; and second, health and local authorities were not always coterminous and it was necessary to determine the representation on JCCs which was best achieved through making them statutory bodies. In addition, many JCCs were large bodies with up to 50 or 60 members. The only statutory requirement on Scottish health boards is that they undertake to collaborate but the mechanism by which they do this has no statutory basis. It is accepted that the SHHD has gone as far as it can without making JLCs statutory. However the situation could change with the passage of the NHS (Amendment) Bill onto the statute book (see below). The Bill received the Royal Assent in October 1986.

The 1977 working party's recommendations were eventually adopted in a circular (SHHD 1980a), published four years after the English equivalent, which gave an undertaking that the arrangements would be reviewed in the light of experience. Such a review was undertaken five years later in April 1985 when the 1980 circular was replaced by new guidance (Scottish Office 1985) which followed nearly a year of consultation. The circular was also motivated by mounting pressure from outside interest groups, particularly from a grouping of some 22 voluntary bodies – the Care in the Community Scottish Working Group – established in 1982 because of a shared concern at the lack of progress in Scotland in the development of a coherent strategy for care in the community and for the chief means to achieve this, namely, joint planning.

The 1985 circular reaffirmed the Secretary of State's objective of promoting closer collaboration between not only health boards and local authorities but also voluntary agencies and other organisations. The circular re-emphasised that boards and authorities have a statutory responsibility to cooperate with one another and that the framework for this in most areas exists in JLCs. But the circular also conceded that in practice cooperation between these bodies and the JLC arrangements 'have not been uniformly successful' (paragraph 4, page 2). In order to 'beef up' existing arrangements the Secretary of State asked that joint plans be prepared for services for the priority categories in *SHAPE*. In the first instance the ten year plans would 'be for the guidance of the health board and the local authorities concerned; they need not be formally submitted to the Secretary of State, and will not require his approval, although it would be helpful if copies were sent to him' (paragraph 6, page 2). The first round of plans were to be drawn up not later than the end of March 1986 and were to be kept under continuing review thereafter. At the time of writing, joint plans from only three health boards (2 island and 1 mainland) – Orkney, Shetland and Lothian – had been received by the SHHD.

Officials in the SHHD were of the opinion that the time had come when, as one expressed it, 'just putting a few pious words on paper was no longer enough'. *Requiring* health and local authorities to collaborate was thought to be necessary. The preparation of joint plans was something for local agencies 'to get their teeth into'. An official acknowledged that the joint plans would inevitably be 'rough and ready' in the first year but this was justified on the grounds of getting some movement.

> If we hadn't set a short time scale, then it would have dragged on and the intention is that they should be reviewed so that they will be refined as experience goes on.

The official went on to admit that the status of the plans was:

> ... a little hazy. They will not be submitted to the Department [that is, the SHHD]; on the other hand, the Department will expect

to see them ... The reason we haven't asked for them to be submitted is because we don't know what we're going to do in the sense that we do not have a separate interdepartmental process for assessing these plans. At present we have two processes, one which is working reasonably in the health service and one which is just beginning to start up in the social work service for assessing health and social work objectives.

In addition, SHHD officials were under pressure as a result of a reduction in staff numbers and other demands on their time. 'We are in no position to demand that these plans be submitted with the implication that there'll be a response to them'. As a result, the joint plans were primarily seen by the centre as informing local agencies' own planning processes. Conceivably the position might be different in two or three years' time with the process becoming more formalised. Progress might hinge upon the outcome of the *SHAPE* review. If *SHAPE*'s successor places a greater emphasis on joint planning then monitoring will become much more concerned with joint planning. The process will gain its own momentum and, in the words of the SHHD official, 'these [joint] plans will become a replacement for separate health and social work plans'. At the present time, however,

... we thought it important just to make sure that there was something ... a crystal round which joint planning could grow because it was clear that without such a crystal it wasn't going to grow.

The scope of the joint plans was deliberately left a little vague for sound pragmatic reasons. As an official from SHHD explained:

... one can imagine that in the early days [the plans] will be restricted to projects which, for one reason or another, benefit from support finance ... Sooner or later I think we shall have to encourage health boards and local authorities to really integrate their service planning over the whole field so that the health board which was contemplating looking at the future of its mental illness services could not do so in isolation. It would have to take the social work authority [and] voluntary agencies with it and discuss *ab initio* what services should be provided for the mentally ill in that area, not whether there should be a new hospital there in [year] but whether there should be a hospital at all.

It was argued that sooner or later joint plans would have to be rooted in a fundamental strategy rather than represent a list of projects,

121

capital or otherwise. A shared philosophy of care between all local agencies was a prerequisite. However, at least one official in the SHHD was convinced that joint planning could not be imposed. 'You can't legislate for effective joint planning ... The English have tried ... put anything onto a statute book, it doesn't make a blind bit of difference at the end of the day unless you get people to actually do something, to appreciate the needs ...' The view was expressed that in England, the DHSS regarded policy implementation as a legitimate role for the centre whereas in Scotland, the SHHD had recognised that responsibility for implementation rested at a local level.

The SHHD's view of joint planning as described above is not widely shared and it has come under increasing pressure, chiefly from outside pressure groups, since the appearance of the circular to put joint planning on the same statutory basis as England and Wales. The campaign culminated in a clause to this effect being inserted in Tom Clarke's Bill to improve service provision for disabled persons. The clause proposed the establishment of a joint planning committee in each health board, but technical difficulties prevented the introduction of a clause to cover the full range of priority groups for which existing joint planning arrangements in Scotland provide. The government therefore introduced an amendment to the NHS (Amendment) Bill which, on becoming an Act, has put into statute a provision identical to that envisaged for the Disabled Persons Bill. The new clause on joint planning in Scotland requires the Scottish Office to put joint planning machinery on a statutory basis if the present voluntary arrangement fails. It will be for the Secretary of State to decide if the voluntary arrangement has failed and whether, therefore, to use his reserve powers. A circular setting out the new reserve powers, and possibly making explicit the criteria governing their use, was in preparation at the time of writing.

The record of joint planning

In contrast to developments in England and Wales, the record of joint planning in Scotland has been remarkable for the virtual absence of any progress. Joint planning is not regarded as an integral part of health care, or social care, planning. It is largely viewed as a 'bolt on' accessory and a non-essential one at that. In part this may be a reflection of the systemic hospital bias described in Chapter 4 but it may also have to do with varying conceptions of planning. While health boards possess *capital* planning skills, *service* planning skills remain weak and underdeveloped. The early experiences of the PPCs bear out this observation. Only in the abstract has service planning been a well practiced art (Hunter 1980; Leary 1983; Brown 1985).

To date, as we noted above, and after passing the deadline of 31 March 1986 for the first round of joint plans, only three health boards have submitted joint plans to the Secretary of State. Other boards are claimed to be moving in the desired direction, albeit at a slower pace than that recommended in the 1985 circular (*Hansard*, Written Answers, 10 April 1986). The key factors constraining progress concern both the commitment on behalf of the two main sets of agencies to collaborate, and the capability to operationalise that commitment where it exists. There are weaknesses in both areas. While joint plans may often amount to little more than lists of projects, they are expected to be rooted sooner or later in a fundamental strategy. SHHD officials concede that this will take time to evolve. Only if both organisations share the same philosophy will projects begin to work. 'If they agree about their philosophy of care and then all the projects they'll almost automatically work out . . . the plan will not exactly write itself but it will tend to write itself . . . but that's some way off.' As we pointed out earlier, the Department does not believe it can impose joint planning. The idea that a policy can be implemented from the centre is nonsense when 'responsibility for its implementation rests at local level'.

The planning capability of health boards is generally under-developed and in regard to joint planning virtually non-existent. This is one factor behind the SHHD's insistence that joint plans be produced for the provision of services for the priority categories identified in *SHAPE*. It is accepted, as mentioned already, that the joint plans, whenever they appear, will neither be easy to produce nor particularly meaningful. The problem in local authorities is possibly more acute when it comes to social services planning, with very few individuals capable of executing such a task.

As mentioned already, for most health boards planning is thought of in terms of capital projects rather than in terms of services. The PPCs which operated in most boards between 1975 and 1979 gave an impetus to service planning and also resulted in collaborative ventures with social work and housing being represented on the committees.

In general, PPCs had no influence on policy at the end of the day (Boddy 1979). Their benefits were indirect, such as fostering cross-sector links. They also gave the priority care groups a certain status within health boards, both raising their profile and partially compensating for their traditional neglect. The PPCs were advisory and had no direct access to the boards, although board members were included in the membership. All reports had to be processed through the management system and officers were anxious not to allow PPCs to get too close to actual decision-making or to disturb their equilibrium.

In the end, the PPCs withered away. Once they had reported there was no further role for them since they had no remit to monitor the implementation of their plans. In most health boards, the committees were not formally abolished but simply went into recess.

For the past six to seven years, there has been little or no joint planning activity in Scotland apart from JLCs which meet, in the main, once or twice a year with officer support groups meeting more often. In the past year or so, there has been a revival of interest in PPCs or some variant of the model underpinning them. As we noted above, this has largely been prompted by the requirement on health boards and local authorities to produce joint plans, but one or two boards were already expressing concern that earlier PPC reports did not seem to be having much impact and ought to be reviewed, updated and their implementation secured. The titles of the various planning groups vary, as does the progress being made, but common features are the virtual (and deliberate) exclusion of board members and the moves to involve voluntary bodies in planning.

Available evidence, both anecdotal and from a variety of research studies and surveys (Hunter 1980; Gray and Hunter 1983; Brown 1985; Care in the Community Scottish Working Group 1986a and 1986b; University of Aberdeen/Loughborough University 1986; Scottish Action on Dementia 1986) shows unequivocally that joint planning has produced few tangible results and that JLCs do not appear to be an effective focus for joint planning. The Care in the Community Scottish Working Group has concluded that in many parts of the country the circular had had little impact and in some none whatever. 'The current state of relative inaction in many areas is ... a sad reflection upon the commitment of health boards and local authorities as well as an indictment of the circular [that is, Scottish Office 1985] itself' (1986a).

In regard to JLCs, the Aberdeen/Loughborough survey found that a higher value was placed on regular officer contact than on the JLC, and the infrequent meetings of JLCs seemed to confirm this view of their worth. It is a view shared by some central government officials and advisers. As one SWSG official explained, officers at local level

> ... can actually achieve things, not quite despite the JLC but certainly outside the boundaries of the JLC, quite effectively limiting what the JLC itself ever deals with. It may deal with loose strategy but the real problem is what happens on a day-to-day basis and if that is handled satisfactorily at different levels by the officer working groups then that is much more effective. For the centre, coterminosity and the fact that Scotland being a small place people tended to know each other better which facilitated cooperation,

were the key features in accounting for cooperative success. However, hard evidence of the beneficial impact of these twin factors is lacking.

In the survey responses there were few comments on the circular's guidance on joint planning. Concern was confined to the revised arrangements for support finance (see Chapter 7).

At a seminar of JLC secretaries in December 1985 organised by the Care in the Community Scottish Working Group (1986b) the conclusion reached was that despite a spate of activity as health boards and local authorities reassessed their joint planning machinery and set up new groups, the new arrangements had yet to bear fruit. Moreover, there were major issues still to be tackled in Scotland such as establishing a clear political commitment to community care at national level in order to provide a supportive environment in which to proceed. This was a quite separate matter from attempts to get the machinery in place. If the political commitment was forthcoming then the machinery would most likely follow.

The Scottish Office claims that it is, over a year later, evaluating the impact of its 1985 circular on joint planning, although quite how this is being achieved remains something of a mystery. The outcome of this review will either be a retention of the voluntary system of joint planning, which is the stated preference of Ministers, or as a concession to external pressure and in keeping with the relevant clause in the NHS (Amendment) Act, a move to put joint planning on a statutory footing. The Secretary of the Scottish Health Service Planning Council is on record as stating that 'we have not developed joint planning with local authority and voluntary bodies'. He told the centenary conference of the Psychiatric Nurses Association Scotland in June 1986 that, as a result, adequate provision had not been made for the priority client groups. He did, however, claim that the picture was changing 'slower than perhaps we would like but definitely altering towards the priority groups'. Evidence of this shift, however gradual, is not available. As we have shown in Chapter 3, past trends do not point to a markedly different future. Whatever the true position, joint planning in Scotland seems to be at the crossroads and events over the next few months are likely to be crucial in determining its future direction.

ARRANGEMENTS FOR COLLABORATION: WALES

Health and local authority structures

From 1974–1982, the basic structural arrangements for promoting health and local authority collaboration in Wales paralleled those in

England. Area health authorities were established on the boundaries of the eight Welsh counties and the same legislation (the 1973 Health Service Reorganisation Act) imposed identical statutory duties for Welsh health and local authorities to collaborate and set up Joint Consultative Committees (JCCs). However, the Welsh Office adopted a less prescriptive approach than the DHSS to the creation of planning machinery to support JCCs. Whereas authorities in England were required in 1976 to establish joint care planning teams of senior officers (DHSS 1976a), the equivalent Welsh Office circular merely invited authorities 'to consider the possible advantages' of, *inter alia*, 'setting up a supporting planning group of officers' in areas where such a mechanism did not exist (Welsh Office 1977, paragraph 5). In a similar vein, the Welsh Secretary recognised the 'scope for a variety of patterns related to the particular circumstances of each area and believe [d] it . . . right to leave the authorities concerned to determine their own particular pattern of supporting planning teams'. The guidance went on to note that authorities would 'need to consider the balance of advantage in deciding whether or not health care planning teams for particular client groups or services should be replaced by or complemented by joint care planning teams'. By contrast, the 1977 DHSS circular emphasised that where health care planning teams had not been abolished following receipt of the previous year's circular, they should be abolished forthwith (DHSS 1977a).

Further differences between England and Wales began to emerge with the 1982 restructuring of the NHS. Although the original consultative document preceding this reorganisation, *Patients First*, bore the joint imprint of the DHSS and the Welsh Office (1979), references to Wales were minimal (paragraphs 2, 46 and 47) and contained proposals which were to some extent at variance with those for England. Certainly its contents gave rise to some 'considerable misunderstanding of the implications of the proposals for Wales', as the Welsh Office acknowledged in a document subsequently issued, in part, to clarify such misunderstandings (Welsh Office 1980, paragraph 4). The essential difference between the two countries was the proposal to establish district health authorities in England and abolish the area tier, but to retain area health authorities in Wales. The suggestion gave rise to an expectation that the overall objective of *Patients First* – the strengthening of management processes at local level – might not be realised in Wales. However, the Secretary of State emphasised that the delegation of authority to new local units of management would apply in Wales no less than in England (page 2).

Thus the fundamental distinction between England and Wales lay in the retention in Wales of health authorities coterminous with local social services authorities. The rationale advanced by the Welsh Office for this structure is interesting. On the one hand, it noted that administrative structures were less strongly established at district level in Wales than in England and that 'considerable extra administrative costs – inevitably at the expense of services to patients – would be incurred in setting up additional health authorities' (Welsh Office 1980, paragraph 21). On the other hand, it argued that in practice the proposed district authorities in England and the area authorities in Wales 'would be broadly similar in terms of resources deployed and population served' (paragraph 4). The last part of that argument is difficult to sustain, however. With the exception of Powys, the Welsh Counties all have populations in excess of 400,000 (and two are greater than half a million) whereas the average size of the new English districts is under 300,000. Equally interesting is the emphasis in Wales on the need to avoid 'the disruption and trauma' of breaking up the existing areas (paragraph 16) and the 'obvious complication in liaison arrangements between AHAs, FPCs and local authorities which would arise from loss of coterminosity' (paragraph 21). Similar arguments, as we noted, underlay the decision to retain area health boards in Scotland.

Patients First had made a similar point in its discussion of the Welsh context: 'there can be no clear prospect that change now in the number or in the boundaries of the present authorities would bring benefits sufficient to outweigh the disruption that this would inevitably cause. The balance of advantage, therefore, lies in stability' (DHSS and Welsh Office 1979, paragraph 47). Thus the 'particular dissatisfaction with the administrative process within the multi district areas' was to be met by abolishing districts rather than areas. Similar arguments were advanced in England before and after the publication of *Patients First* but they carried little weight and it is difficult to know how far the relative weakness of existing district administrative structures in Wales constituted the only real reason for Wales not following England in this respect. Whatever the case, the 1982 restructuring proceeded along different lines in Wales with the emphasis on minimising disruption to health and local authority collaboration through the retention of coterminosity. (Only in Dyfed was local pressure successful in creating new authorities from existing districts). As a result, it might prove instructive to explore whether changes in internal management processes have been introduced at least as effectively in Wales as in England and without the additional costs of upheaval associated with structural change. Nonetheless, on the evidence available, it is not clear that the absence of disruption to the structures associated with health and local authority joint planning has enabled cooperative working to advance any more smoothly than – or even to the same extent as – in England.

The record of joint planning

Evidence about collaboration between Welsh health and local authorities is scanty. Although the national surveys of 1982 and 1984 included Wales, the level of returns was too small for meaningful analysis. Given the relatively high response rate in England for each of the surveys (79 per cent and 74 per cent), this experience may itself suggest a lower degree of interest in collaboration within the Principality. Certainly, our interviews with officials in the Welsh Office revealed a perception that local joint planning was underdeveloped both generally and in comparison with England. The advent of the All Wales Strategy for mentally handicapped people was, however, seen to be making some impact on the need to strengthen planning relationships between health and local authorities.

The view from Cardiff was that local joint planning existed at different levels of development. In a minority of localities, personality factors loomed large and it was considered that 'just getting them to talk would be a major step forward'. In other cases, the perception was of an established framework which would allow an advance to be made: 'we've got the tool, we've got the joint planning groups ... we've got people who are really switched on'. The more general picture, however, was of a situation in which commitment to and understanding of joint planning had been low, at least until very recently. There had been 'confusion between consultation and joint planning. (Local agencies) say, "Oh well, we consulted them" – and that, they thought, was joint planning'. The All Wales Strategy was seen to have made a significant difference. An official suggested that health and local authorities had hitherto:

> ... all nodded towards joint planning ... [they] said 'Yes, joint planning is an excellent thing' – but they very rarely entered into any *real* joint planning, not until circumstances forced it ... particularly the mental handicap Strategy. That's the one thing that's really sharpened up joint planning. It wasn't effective [before]; they would go their own sweet way and say, 'Well, here's our plan, have a look at it and if you agree, that's joint planning'.

More specifically, the Strategy had provided the Welsh Office with leverage to secure joint planning at local level. For the first time, health and local authorities were being required to submit a joint plan for a specific client group and resources could be withheld by the centre unless the plan showed evidence of genuine joint planning. Our respondents argued that these were real powers:

> We've said 'sorry, you are not getting any money until you can show us that you've jointly planned a new service'. And that's

128

concentrated minds and the most dramatic example is (county name) where we had a plan produced which showed absolutely no evidence of joint planning ... We told them 'you can't have the money for this plan; it's not good enough; it doesn't show you are producing a genuinely jointly planned service'. They made a great fuss about it ... They went away – road to Damascus – started consulting vigorously and then produced an absolutely first class plan in the end with the help of parents' groups, and it is a genuine joint plan.

While the influence of the Strategy and of its mechanisms for ensuring collaboration were generally acknowledged, opinion in the Welsh Office differed as to its effect on joint planning across the board. One view was that the Strategy's influence on joint planning was 'double-edged. So much effort has gone into ... [it] that it's arguable [whether] it's leaving a lot of effort for joint planning in other areas'. Even so, it was accepted that there might be benefits for other client groups in the longer term as health and local authorities became accustomed – and actually learned how – to work together and towards a specific set of objectives. The other view was that although 'the other sectors are more ragged', progress was still being made for the other dependency groups. Much remains to be done, however, before joint planning across the board is given the same degree of attention as that for mentally handicapped people.

This impression is confirmed by the reports of the Health Advisory Service (HAS) on their visits to Welsh authorities. Four such reports have been published since HAS reports became publically available in 1985 (Health Advisory Service and Social Work Service of the Welsh Office 1985a, b, c; 1986). Covering four of the eight Welsh social services authorities and five of the nine health authorities, they present a picture of limited progress in joint planning for the elderly (in three cases) and the mentally ill (one case). In Gwent, the HAS concluded that there was 'little evidence that (the JCC and officer) arrangements for cooperation have been successful in stimulating joint planning for the elderly beyond the submission of schemes to the Welsh Office for joint finance' (Health Advisory Service and Social Work Service of the Welsh Office 1985b, paragraph 154). In Powys, the situation was apparently even less favourable with the 'confidence of officers to plan cooperatively ... [not being] assisted when financial commitments undertaken, when joint projects are approved, are later not accepted by one of the parties...' (Health Advisory Service and Social Work Service of the Welsh Office 1986, paragraph 144). Indeed, the Powys report went so far as to make reference to the need for 'the credibility of joint care planning ... to be salvaged' (paragraph 145). In South

Glamorgan, the HAS indicated that little real progress had been made, emphasising that 'both Authorities need a more effective mechanism for agreeing joint objectives, reaching agreement on a joint strategy for change, and providing realistic resource guidelines to their officers' (1985c, paragraph 230). The same report also suggested the existence of scepticism about the value of joint planning and noted this arose from approaching it as 'something only concerned with the best way of using a marginal amount of additional resources' (paragraph 229).

Taken together, the HAS reports on experience at local level provide a strong counterpoint to the Welsh Office's perception of the impact of the All Wales Strategy on planning for mentally handicapped people. Little if any evidence emerges of effective joint planning for elderly or mentally ill people and in some cases relationships appear to be negative rather than merely under-developed or lacking in commitment (see not only the Powys example above but also the case of Gwent where the HAS described as an 'urgent objective' the 'Health Authority's hope that effective joint planning arrangements' could be developed with social services and housing (1985b, paragraph 7). Highly unusually, however, the county council had not participated in the HAS visit. As in South Glamorgan (1985c, paragraph 229), the Gwent report noted that 'joint planning is unlikely to be successful if it is perceived as undermining the independence of the statutory authorities to manage and develop their individual services instead of enhancing their ability to make the best use of their own resources' (1985b, paragraph 154). Given this apparently low level of achievement, it will be important to monitor whether recent policy and financial initiatives for the elderly – which in some respects parallel the All Wales Strategy – lead to significant improvements in inter-agency planning and relationships for this client group.

SUMMARY

What emerges most clearly from our review and assessment of joint planning across Britain is that progress has been limited and uneven. In none of the three countries has collaborative planning achieved the results sought when the NHS and local government were reorganised in the mid-1970s. Comprehensive joint planning for individual client groups has been rare though there are strong indications that, in the case of mental handicap, this is beginning to take off universally in Wales. Successful collaborative ventures have, however, occurred more frequently around individual projects especially in England and Wales. In Scotland, on the other hand, where the first circular on joint planning did not appear until 1980, both practice and debate are less

130

advanced. In particular, and akin to the early discussions in England and Wales, there appears to be a somewhat naive belief that the key to effective joint planning lies in getting the structure right. The experience in England and Wales suggests that this view is misplaced and that process factors are at least as important.

In England the *Progress in Partnership* working party is indicative of a reawakening at national level of an interest in joint planning which seemed to wane with the publication of *Patients First* in 1979 and the subsequent restructuring of the NHS. Nonetheless, while its report gives more attention to processes necessary for successful joint planning, its predominant perspective remains a narrowly rational and managerialist one. The report makes valuable recommendations for strengthening both collaborative structures and accountability processes but gives insufficient attention to the essentially political skills of inter-agency bargaining and negotiation so vital to successful inter-agency planning.

The development and deployment of such skills are critical issues for policy-makers in each of the three countries. Related to this is the need for incentives to encourage joint working. Both the experience of the All Wales Strategy and of joint support finance suggest the important contribution of financial incentives. In the next chapter we review more specifically the evolution and operation of joint/support finance in promoting collaboration.

Chapter 7
INTER-SERVICE COLLABORATION AT LOCAL LEVEL
2   FINANCIAL INCENTIVES

INTRODUCTION

The importance of financial arrangements for implementing community care policies was emphasised in Chapter 3. Our argument was that the development of new service structures depends on the capacity of the centre to ensure that resource flows are congruent with the shifts in the balance of agency responsibilities envisaged by such policies. We also commented on the extent to which the block grants potentially provide scope for the Scottish and Welsh Offices to harmonise policies for services and resources compared with the situation in England. Similar financial considerations arise at the level of health and local authorities. National policies for community care have implied a proportionately greater role for local authorities (especially that of their social services departments): more prosaically, they impose additional demands on local rate-borne expenditure while apparently reducing the call on centrally funded health services. Even in a period of relative plenty, such a proposition was unattractive to many local authorities (Parker 1965). Prolonged financial famine has only served to sharpen these difficulties, although central government has sought to meet them through the introduction of financial incentives for local authorities to assume the role required of them.

These arrangements, known as joint finance in England and Wales and support finance in Scotland, were initially designed to encourage social services departments to engage in collaborative planning with health authorities by providing earmarked funds to pump prime service developments which benefited the NHS. Subsequently, they were modified to include housing, education and voluntary agencies within their remit. The levels of resources available under the joint/ support finance schemes vary between the three countries. In Scotland and Wales the level of funding has been considerably more modest when compared with England (see Table 7).

In addition to these limited earmarked funds, complementary transfer arrangements have enabled health authorities to make payments from their mainstream budgets to such bodies and without time limit. In the following sections we examine differences in the

132

Table 7 **Amounts available for allocation from central funds 1980/81 to 1985/86**

	1980/81	*1981/82*	*1982/83*	*1983/84*	*1984/85*	*1985/86*
Gross £m						
England	61.0	75.3	84.7	94.1★	99.5	105.0
Scotland	1.0	1.1	2.0	3.2★	4.6	6.0
Wales	0.5	0.6	1.1	1.2	1.6	1.4
Per capita £						
England	1.31	1.62	1.81	2.01	2.11	2.23
Scotland	0.19	0.21	0.39	0.63	0.89	1.15
Wales	0.18	0.21	0.39	0.43	0.57	0.50

★ Reduced from £96 m and £3.6 m respectively following the Chancellor's announcement on 9 July 1983.

Source: Department of Health and Social Security, Scottish Home and Health Department and Welsh Office

timing, scale, and experience of operating such financial arrangements in England, Scotland and Wales respectively (see also Table 8).

FINANCIAL INCENTIVES FOR COMMUNITY CARE: ENGLAND

The DHSS took an early lead in introducing joint finance in 1976. Equivalent developments did not take place in Wales until the following year and it was not until 1980 that the Scottish support finance scheme got under way. In England, the initiative reflected a keen ministerial commitment to promote collaboration and to reduce the scale of long-stay hospital provision (Castle 1975). Its essential features may be summarised as follows:

1 The DHSS 'top sliced' the NHS budget to provide health authorities with earmarked funds to support selected personal social services capital and revenue expenditure.

2 The funds were allocated to regional health authorities and then to district health authorities in accordance with formulae which reflect characteristics of the population served including numbers in the dependency groups.

3 The sums involved were relatively small, building up from minimal levels to a total equivalent to only some 1 per cent of NHS and 3 per cent of personal social services planned spending in 1985/86.

133

4   The criterion to be applied by health authorities in allocating these funds was that their expenditure 'could be expected to make a better contribution in terms of total care than would deployment of equivalent resources directly on health services' (DHSS 1976a).

5   Such sums could be used to support social services schemes for only limited periods (a maximum of five years, initially) and on a tapering basis: as NHS payments were reduced social services departments were required to make their own contributions to joint finance schemes until the full costs were met from their own budgets.

6   Joint finance could not be diverted into mainstream NHS ac-tivities; unspent monies had to be carried forward with the next year's allocation or returned to the regional health authority. (Subsequently, and providing the local authority was agreeable, health authorities were permitted to use joint finance to support certain primary and community health services; however, acute hospital services could not be financed from this source. Joint finance was available to the NHS only on the same pump priming basis as applied to support for social services expenditure).

Since 1976, the fundamental features of the joint finance arrangements have remained basically unchanged. However, the history of joint finance has been marked by certain relaxations in the conditions under which it might be spent. Details of this increased flexibility are provided in Table 8. They have been essentially concerned with extending both the range of agencies whose services might be supported from the joint finance allocation and also the period for which such support might be paid. These modifications in part reflected an acceptance that joint finance might appropriately pump prime the full range of services involved in providing community care. However, the financial climate in which the programme operated has been a more immediate factor in determining NHS access to this source of funds and also the introduction of longer periods of revenue support.

It is axiomatic that, as a source of short-term funding, joint finance is dependent on the availability of growth in mainstream budgets if it is to be of lasting benefit. Yet, joint finance was introduced at precisely the time when social services growth rates were being revised downwards to 2 per cent per annum following a brief period of double digit growth (Webb and Wistow 1982). Apparently as a result of local authority reluctance to overcommit themselves in such circumstances, the proportion of joint finance taken up in the first two years (1976/77 and 1977/8) was only 52 per cent and 75 per cent (Wistow 1983). The

134

result was the introduction of terms designed to make joint finance more attractive to social services departments and local authority treasurers: 100 per cent rather than 60 per cent became the norm for initial levels of support with tapering thereafter taking place over a seven rather than a five year period (DHSS 1977b). At the same time, David Ennals, as Secretary of State for Social Services, positively encouraged health authorities (DHSS 1977a) to use unallocated sums of joint finance to fund certain of the improvements in community services recommended in the report of the Court committee on child health (Parliament 1976). For health authorities, whose growth allocations were already stretched to meet the revenue consequences of long planned district general hospital programmes, this new provision was a welcome, albeit limited, source of financial flexibility.

The effectiveness of joint finance

Evaluations of joint finance have tended to revolve around three related issues: whether it has been spent at all; whether it has been spent productively and cost effectively; and whether it has promoted collaborative planning. In the first instance the balance of concern, both centrally and locally, was to ensure that the allocation was fully taken up. After the relatively low take up rates of the early years, expenditure built up rapidly and health authorities are now planning to spend sums equivalent to almost all the national joint finance allocation (though there are considerable regional variations). By 1985 the cumulative national take up rate for the allocation since its inception in 1976 stood at 98 per cent (House of Commons Social Services Committee 1985, pages 42–44).

Whether such sums have been 'well spent' is more problematic, and is not unrelated to the initial low take up rates. In the early years, at least, most joint finance projects emerged from social services rather than from joint planning processes and were readily accepted by health authorities anxious to restrict the amounts of unspent monies to be carried forward at the year end (Wistow and Head 1981; Wistow 1983). Since such unspent sums were included within the 1 per cent of their revenue allocation that they were allowed to carry forward, health authorities effectively had an incentive not to impose too rigorous a review of the contribution to health service objectives which social services schemes represented. To do otherwise threatened the flexibility which the 1 per cent carry forward facility offered them in planning their main allocation. On the worst scenario, some proportion of such mainstream health monies might be lost to the Exchequer.

Such considerations, together with the technical difficulties of establishing that joint finance schemes represented no less value to the

135

Table 8 Comparison between arrangements for joint finance (England and Wales) and support finance (Scotland)

	1 England	2 England	3 Scotland	4 Scotland	5 Wales	6 Wales
Introduction	1976	Major revision 1983	1980	Revised 1985	1977	Revised 1983
Scope	PSS, voluntary organisations (from 1977), primary and community health (from 1977)	From 1.4.84 – PSS, housing, education, voluntary organisations, primary and community health	Social work, voluntary organisations	From 1.4.85 – social work, voluntary organisations, housing, education	PSS, voluntary organisations	As England (column 2)
Capital payments	60% contribution 'might be a reasonable figure' but higher contributions (up to and including 100%) may be made.	No hard and fast rule; in normal circumstances should not exceed 2/3 of the total cost, but higher contributions up to and including 100% may be made.	Generally not more than 60% of total cost, although 'there may be occasions where a higher contribution might be appropriate'.	As England (column 2)	As England (column 1)	As England (column 2) except normally 50% of final cost.
Revenue payments						
Time limit	Initially not more than 5 years; may be extended by 1–2 years.	*Joint finance schemes:* up to and including 100% for up to 3 years; tapering off over more than a further 4 years; may be extended for a further 1 or 2 years with Secretary of State approval.	Initially, not more than 5 years; may be extended by 1–2 years.	As England (column 2) except that SHHD should be informed of all instances where there has been an extension.	As England (column 1)	As England (column 2) but flexibility can be shown if justified.
Limit of contribution	No hard and fast rule; contributions may be up to 100%. But if the initial	*Care in the Community* (schemes for people moving from hospital to community care) a. Payments from joint finance monies: up to and including 100% for 3 years; tapering off	Generally not more than 60% of project cost in the first year; must taper off (the tapering pattern is not prescribed but is usually a 10% a year reduction)	a. 100% of project cost for up to 3 years. Thereafter tapering off (pattern not prescribed) over no more than a further	As a general rule initial contribution 60%. In some cases a higher level of support is possible but	As England (column 2) for (a) and (b) except Welsh Office contributes 50% of health service contribution; health authorities match this from their own main

(continued)	more than 60% norm, tapering may be sharper. over no more than a further 4 years. In special circumstances, 100% for 10 years, and payments of less than 100% for a further 3 years. b. Payments from health authorities' normal allocations: up to 100% indefinitely (subject in due course to a central transfer of resources).		4 years. b. Lump sum or continuing payments by health board to local authorities to facilitate transfers from hospital to community (arrangements not prescribed) – may be subject in due course to permanent transfer of resources.	with sharper tapering. allocations; earmarking of NHS funds in Welsh Office in respect of the development of community based services for mentally handicapped people over a period of ten years.	
Allocation made by	DHSS makes allocation to RHAs on a *per capita* basis, weighted to take account of the numbers of mentally ill, mentally handicapped and the over 75s. RHAs allocate to DHAs normally under similar formula.	Same as column 1.	SHHD makes allocation to health boards distributed under SHARE formula. Department indicates a minimum sum which it expects each board to devote to projects. The indicative allocation to be based on population of area, weighted to account for those in need of long term care. SHHD, which evaluates bids from health boards for allocations in respect of specific projects.	As Scotland (column 3) but Welsh Office provides 50% of health service contribution; health authorities match this from their own main allocations.	Same as column 5.
Joint planning arrangements	All projects must be approved by the appropriate joint consultative committee.	Same as column 1.	No formal role for (non-statutory) joint liaison committees (JLCs).	Same as column 3, although joint plans to be prepared by JLCs.	Same as column 1.

NHS than if such sums were spent on health services, tended to mean that joint finance largely supported the kinds of services that social services departments might have developed in any case. Significantly, a national survey of health authorities conducted in 1982 found only 14 per cent reporting that joint finance had enabled them to influence social services department priorities (Wistow and Fuller 1983, page 25). The impact of resource scarcity on local authorities was also seen to be influential: 44 per cent of respondents in the same survey recorded that joint finance had been used predominantly to cushion from the effects of expenditure constraint developments planned separately by social services departments. By 1983, when the Public Accounts Committee examined the operation of joint finance, concern was growing that both DHSS and health authority control of, and accountability for, these monies was proving less than fully adequate. The Committee's concern embraced both the initial appraisal and subsequent monitoring of joint finance projects. In particular, it drew attention to work by the Comptroller and Auditor General's staff suggesting that:

> ... generally health authorities did not hold documentation show-ing that full consideration had been given to NHS as well as to local authority priorities in the choice of scheme; or that there had been an evaluation of the scheme's objectives, likely costs and expected benefits to the NHS. Further, health authorities did not obtain comprehensive information from local authorities enabling them to monitor the implementation of schemes and the benefits accruing to the NHS. (House of Commons Committee of Public Accounts 1983a, paragraph 4).

Given such evidence, the Committee recorded its 'doubts as to how far ... NHS money was being efficiently spent in the interests of the health service' (paragraph 10). Partly in anticipation of the Commit-tee's report and partly because of similar concerns within the Department, the DHSS had already specified more detailed proce-dures for approving and monitoring the use of joint finance (DHSS 1983b). At a policy level, another response to these concerns was for the DHSS to link joint finance more closely with its objectives for the rundown of long-stay hospitals under the terms of the 'care in the community' initiative.

The 'care in the community' initiative

The vast majority of joint finance was allocated by social services departments to the dependency groups at the interface with health

138

services. Children's services – where the overlap with health was less extensive – were allocated relatively little joint finance. In this sense, therefore, joint finance had certainly contributed towards maintaining the development of community services in areas closest to NHS interests (just as the top slicing of joint finance had insulated a portion of the NHS growth budget from the demands of the acute sector). Nonetheless, such services had been, at best, of indirect benefit to the NHS by delaying or preventing hospital admissions. They had not directly contributed to the more rapid rundown of long-stay hospitals by enabling existing patients to be transferred to local authority care and the resulting spare NHS capacity taken out of commission (Wistow 1983; House of Commons Committee of Public Accounts 1983a). Moreover, joint finance was seen as too limited in its scale and period of support for it to make possible a direct and permanent switch in responsibilities for patients with no further need of a hospital bed.

Such considerations came together in the 'care in the community' arrangements (DHSS 1983b), the principal features of which included:

1   Health authorities were permitted to make lump sum or continuing payments from their main allocations for as long as necessary to enable people to be transferred from hospital.

2   The joint finance arrangements were made more flexible by extending the maximum period of joint finance support to 13 years (including 10 at 100 per cent) but only for those schemes which enabled patient transfers to take place. In all other cases, the maximum period was seven years (three at 100 per cent).

It is too early to make a final judgement on the effectiveness of this attempt to refocus financial incentives – and joint planning – on the closure of long-stay hospitals. In the first year, only limited progress was made, as might have been expected given the potentially protracted nature of the negotiations necessary to offset such patient and resource transfers (Wistow and Fuller 1986). Of more fundamental concern, however, is evidence suggesting that health authorities might seek to develop community care models within the NHS rather than agree transfers to local authorities (Wistow and Hardy 1986). Such evidence is reinforced by the trend shown in financial returns made to the DHSS for health authorities to spend increasing proportions of 'their' joint finance allocation on health services (Working Group on Joint Planning 1985). Indeed, NHS spending of joint finance appears to have doubled in the period since 1981/82, having reached almost 20 per cent of all joint finance expenditure by 1984/85 (Wistow and Fuller 1986, page 44).

At the time of writing, therefore, it is by no means clear that either of the financial mechanisms devised to enable local shifts in the balance of care are currently serving that purpose as fully as hoped. Ironically, there are signs that social services dominance over joint finance allocation processes may have been replaced by an emerging NHS dominance. A more even balance of incentives and influence may yet need to be devised if both patients and resources are to move in the direction so long envisaged in national policies for the dependency groups.

Joint finance and joint planning

Implicit in our discussion of the tendency for social services priorities to determine – at least into the early 1980s – the direction of joint finance spending is the programme's lack of success in promoting collaborative planning. As one of us has concluded elsewhere, the essence of joint planning might be considered to imply the modification of agencies' priorities to meet common goals (Wistow and Fuller 1983, page 28). Given the apparent failure of joint finance to align social services priorities more closely with NHS ones, its contribution to joint planning might appear minimal. A similar message is contained within our earlier discussion (Chapter 6) of the generally disappointing record of joint planning to date. The fact that genuine joint planning scarcely exists on the ground suggests that joint finance has been an ineffective vehicle for encouraging inter-agency partnerships in planning. Indeed, as one of us has argued, decisions about spending joint finance could be so time consuming that insufficient attention was directed to more fundamental and long-term planning issues (Wistow 1980; 1982). On this analysis, joint finance has, in effect, 'crowded out' joint planning. Other observers have gone further, suggesting that joint finance could sometimes be a negative influence which placed strain on collaborative relationships and caused health authorities to mistrust local government (Norton and Rogers 1981; Booth 1981). There is also some evidence that the growing awareness that the NHS had failed to exercise an appropriate degree of influence over joint finance spending led the new districts to assert themselves after 1982 (Jasp Team 1984). This, in turn, may have contributed to the NHS seeking to increase its own share of the 'cake' in recent years rather than attempting to modify social services priorities.

Nonetheless, it is important to emphasise that the influence of joint finance on inter-authority relationships has not been wholly negative, nor even wholly neutral. There is general agreement among practitioners (Wistow and Head 1981; Wistow and Fuller 1983; Jasp Team 1984) that joint finance has been a major factor in promoting closer relationships between health and local authorities. If such relationships had not evolved into collaborative planning, they had, nonetheless, formed the basis for a much fuller exchange of information and a much deeper understanding of the systems and constraints within which the respective authorities operated.

Without the need to meet and agree a joint finance programme, such inter-authority learning processes might have been much less fully developed. In addition, joint finance has provided some flexibility for funding new developments. While the majority of the resources appear to have been used to fund traditional kinds of services, a minority have been used to develop useful innovations, initially on a pilot basis, and for which mainstream budgetary support might have been more difficult to secure (National Association of Health Authorities 1982; Glennerster and others 1983). As with joint planning, the best interim judgement would seem to be that if the achievements of joint finance have been more modest than originally intended, the initial expectations may have been too ambitious given what is known about the range and depth of the barriers to inter-agency planning.

FINANCIAL INCENTIVES FOR COMMUNITY CARE: SCOTLAND

Origins and objectives

Support finance, as joint finance is known, did not get under way in Scotland until 1980, four years or so after its introduction in England. The reason for the delay offered by the then Secretary of the SHHD before the Public Accounts Committee (PAC) in January 1983 was that health boards had expressed reservations about support finance and it took some time before a consensus view emerged which enabled a viable scheme to be launched (House of Commons Committee on Public Accounts 1983b). There is certainly some truth in this reasoning because a number of areas in Scotland did not approve of support finance and refused to touch it. In particular, several local authorities, including the largest region in Scotland, Strathclyde, were firmly opposed to it on political grounds. Their view was that support finance would, in effect, pre-empt, and distort, the priorities of the regions in years to come. Consequently between 1980 and 1985, when the method of allocation was revised (see below and Table 8), take-up across the country varied markedly. This worked to the advantage of some health boards, particularly Highland, which were able to lay their hands on quite sizeable sums of money.

The objectives of support finance are virtually the same as those applying to England. In Sir Kenneth Stowe's (Permanent Secretary, DHSS) words, the mechanism 'was conceived as an instrument to bring about more effective joint planning between local authorities and health authorities' (House of Commons Committee on Public Accounts 1983b, page 1). In the case of Scotland, support finance was viewed as a mechanism which might help ensure that the priority care groups identified in *SHAPE* received the most appropriate form of care with the emphasis on non-institutional provision in the community. Perhaps in Scotland even more than in England the pump priming nature of support finance has been preserved and stressed. Hence the view that the scheme should not normally provide for grants of more than 60 per cent (this was changed to 100 per cent in 1985 – see below). Support finance was seen as experimental and limited in scope. As an SHHD official put it, if an idea worked 'it'll be taken onto a mainstream budget of whatever sort'. However, SHHD efforts 'to be rational about all this were rather submerged by the tremendous political pressure we were under' to imitate England where the original notion of pump priming was 'almost immediately forgotten in the sort of trendy notion of developing community care at the expense of the health service because the English saw mileage in tranferring people from hospital to community care'. In Scotland the directors of social work maintained that 'the grass is greener on the other side (that is, England) and they've got lots of money sloshing around'. Pressure groups were also set up, like the umbrella organisation representing a number of voluntary bodies, the Care in the Community Scottish Working Group. An SHHD official maintained that 'it's very difficult for government departments to resist that sort of pressure entirely and sooner or later the Minister feels that he has to buy them off'. On this occasion, a decision was made to buy time and to concentrate on joint planning (see Chapter 6). Unless sizeable sums of money were available 'we were never going to be in a position to achieve a radical redirection of social work priorities with health service money. It was more important to use support finance "to oil the wheels" but much more important to make sure that the wheels were all going in the same direction ... so that the priority client groups weren't left out'. This, then, is the official explanation for a stress on joint planning and a refusal to regard support finance as a substitute for reallocating main budgets to jointly agreed developments. Indeed, SHHD officials would be quite prepared to see support finance disappear and simply become part of the total allocation of a health board which it now virtually is. Support finance does not enjoy a high profile under the post 1985 arrangements. As one SHHD official explained: 'why should we make a distinction between a new hospital, a support finance project, more nurses or

142

whatever? They are all options that a health board has to evaluate'.

The discrepancy between the amounts of money available in Scotland and England (see Table 7) is officially explained as being partly due to the fact that the Scottish arrangements were not introduced until four years after those in England and the Scottish scheme had not accumulated a correspondingly large number of continuing projects. Although the initial *per capita* level of support finance in Scotland was similar to the corresponding figure when the English scheme was introduced in 1976, it has not increased as rapidly over the years as the respective figures in Table 7 show (£0.63 *per capita* in Scotland in 1983/84, that is, four years after the introduction of support finance, compared with £1.00 *per capita* in England in 1979/80 after four years). To achieve parity with England on a *pro rata* basis would require an additional £12 to £13 million. As one SWSG official explained 'we started where England started instead of starting where England had got to in the four years'. A further reason was the difficulty in justifying large increases in the overall amount available when in the first four years the rate of take-up was slow. There was also some resistance to top-slicing too generously since the greater the amounts taken off the top of the general health service budget for support finance, the smaller the amounts available to health boards for general revenue distribution thus reducing, on a geographically arbitrary basis, the scope for local decisions on resource allocation. Unlike England, therefore, Scotland did not opt for large annual increases in the early years.

The development of support finance

Columns 3 and 4 in Table 8 show the key features of support finance and the revisions over its six-year lifespan. Support finance started life under far tighter central control over its management and distribution than existed in England (columns 1 and 2). In this respect it resembled the mechanism in Wales (columns 5 and 6). From 1980 until 1985 funds top-sliced from the NHS vote were retained by the SHHD and the 15 health boards were invited to submit bids. Support finance, then, was a rare example of a centrally earmarked fund. Initially the view was that the scheme should not provide for grants of more than 60 per cent of the capital and/or initial revenue cost of a particular project or service. The local authority had to meet the balance normally increasing to the full long-term cost after no more than five years as health board revenue support tapered off. The 60 per cent contribution from support finance was, however, subject to some flexibility in practice.

Since its introduction, support finance has steadily increased as the amount top-sliced off normal health board allocations has grown. Despite this growth the take-up of funds between 1980 and 1985 was disappointing. As mentioned, Strathclyde Region and subsequently Lothian Region found support finance unacceptable until very recently. Between them the two regions cover the bulk of Scotland's population. So although the majority of regional and island councils participated in the scheme most of the population was denied any of the alleged benefits of support finance. Nevertheless, the take-up of support finance grew modestly each year from its introduction. Take-up in 1980/81 was 41 per cent compared with 90 per cent in 1984/85, the final year before changes were made in the system of allocation (see below). The rapid increase in take-up in later years may have reflected the resource famine across the public sector which left support finance as a less unattractive source of 'new' money. Moreover, the boycott of support finance by the two largest regions meant the availability of more funds for the remaining regions.

It is not clear why the centre in Scotland assumed more control over the allocation of support finance than the centre in England. While it was in keeping with the SHHD's role in managing aspects of the Scottish Health Service in ways akin to an English RHA, it was certainly not in keeping with its preference for a 'hands off' relationship. It is almost certain that this view of its relationship with health boards was one of the factors which finally led the SHHD to introduce a major change in the arrangements from 1985/86. It had also been a major factor in the delay in the introduction of support finance. Earmarking was not popular with officials. The SHHD did not want to introduce the scheme because, in the words of an official in the SWSG, it meant 'creaming money off the health boards budgets to create a fund to operate the scheme' which was not popular with boards. The four years between the start of joint finance in England and support finance in Scotland were spent 'trying to decide whether or not we should create a fund and the basis for doing it'. Had health boards opted to transfer resources voluntarily then support finance would not have been introduced. But the central department was under growing pressure to act. As an SHHD official conceded:

> Left to ourselves I don't think we would have gone down the slide. It's a very messy business . . . and a somewhat pointless business at the end of the day tranferring resources at the local level. But it had been invented unfortunately and therefore there was a strong pressure on us from the lobby groups to follow the English initiative and we introduced the scheme on a fairly limited basis and it grew steadily.

144

It seems, too, that the scheme introduced in 1980 operated differently from that set out in the circular. According to the SHHD official

> ... the circular talked about, in effect, health boards just ringing the Department up and we would put the cheque in the post to them, that we would have a fund and we would simply give it out in response to bids but in fact what we always did was exercise very close control over the nature of the projects ... It meant that the Department was entirely in control of the objectives of support finance and there were a lot of projects that were referred back either because they didn't have enough information or we thought they were more appropriate for joint finance* or we didn't like them at all or we thought they were too expensive.

A further reason for a central bidding system was given by the Welsh Office to the PAC and it is possible that this may also have been a factor in Scotland although never explicitly articulated. Given the small amounts of joint finance available in Wales, to have allocated them to health authorities according to a formula would have meant that there would be little scope for backing particularly imaginative but relatively expensive projects. In Scotland there is concern that the revised arrangements introduced in 1985 will have precisely this effect although it is too early to pass judgement on whether or not this will prove to be a genuine worry.

To date support finance has primarily benefited elderly people and mentally handicapped people (figures for years 1980/81 to 1983/84 are given in Table 9). There have been very few projects for mentally ill people although this is one of the *SHAPE* category A priority groups. The SHHD's policy has not been to encourage health boards to favour one client group in preference to others. Its view has always been that the choice of projects is for local decision. A further explanation for a relative neglect of the mentally ill could be the absence of a coherent mental health policy in Scotland which is likely to be reflected in a lack of activity at local level. A Planning Council report (SHHD and SED 1985) on mental health services appeared belatedly in 1985, ten years after the programme planning group to prepare it had been set up (Drucker 1986). The official SHHD view is that the lack of projects for the mentally ill might in part be because community care for this group could primarily involve health service support, through the community health services, rather than local authority provision and therefore would not be eligible for support finance.

---

* Joint finance in Scotland has a quite specific meaning. In such cases, NHS and local authority finance may be used for jointly planned and managed projects.

Table 9 **Proportion of support finance allocated to client groups 1980/81 to 1983/84**

	1980/81 %	*1981/82* %	*1982/83* %	*1983/84* %	*% Allocation over 4 years*
Physically/mentally handicapped	28	19	29	59	41
Mentally ill	10	–	–	–	–
Elderly	29	73	44	33	40
Other	33	7	27	8	17

Source: Scottish Home and Health Department.

The arrangements for support finance were actually revised in 1984, although the circular announcing the changes did not appear until April 1985 (Scottish Office 1985). The review was prompted by the DHSS's review of joint finance in 1983 and by growing unease within the SHHD over administering the bidding system which was becoming increasingly onerous as the sums of money grew and take-up increased. The 'self-inflicted monitoring' arrangements were not thought to be an effective use of scarce staff resources. As one official in the SHHD explained, the system was 'administratively a very tiresome business'. There was also pressure for change building up outside the Scottish Office among pressure groups representing voluntary interests, and among local authorities. Few, however, were wholly satisfied with the resulting system of indicative allocations which was likely to mean less joint activity rather than more. In seeking a revised system, local authorities wanted more generous terms but a retention of central control. Their wishes were not realised.

The changes were founded on the assumption that more effective local collaboration could best be encouraged by the removal, as far as possible, of intervention from the centre in the joint deliberations of health boards and local authorities. Local authority and voluntary interests complained that the terms on which support finance was made available were insufficiently attractive, particularly by comparison with the more generous terms introduced in 1983 by the DHSS and the Welsh Office. The new circular did not fully meet these reservations. There was still concern that the principle of earmarked funds had been lost from view and that an absence of central control would allow intransigence or evasion by health boards. It remains to be seen what the outcome of the revised arrangements will be; not much progress was expected in the first year.

Initially the view taken by the SHHD, after consultation with the interests involved, was that all responsibility for operating support finance should be devolved to health boards. Boards would receive their full financial allocations (with no top-slicing) and would be free to transfer resources to local authorities to meet the capital and/or revenue costs of particular projects. The selection of projects, the proportion of project costs met from health services finance, and the period over which payment might be made, would be entirely for local agreement between health boards and the relevant local authorities. However, ministers were of the opinion that this was perhaps going too far and that the centre should retain some means of influencing the amounts spent on support finance and the uses to which the funds were put. Consequently, the circular states that the Scottish Office should disengage itself completely from day-to-day involvement in the operation of support finance but that the SHHD should give each health board a non-mandatory indication of the sum which it expects it to devote to support finance projects from within the normal revenue allocations. The indicative allocation, based on the population of the area, weighted to account for those in need of long-term care, represents a minimum sum for each health board. Boards are free to exceed this indicative allocation if they wish. Presumably they can also direct the indicative allocation to other purposes if they wish since there is no obligation on them to use it to fund projects with local authorities. However, the SHHD has said that it will know of the use made of these resources both as a result of monitoring the progress made towards implementing the *SHAPE* recommendations and through receiving copies of memoranda recording the agreements made between health boards and local authorities.

In addition to disengagement by the centre the other major change is a widening of the scope of support finance to include appropriate housing and education initiatives and thereby bring practice into line with that in England. Also, the flexibility of support finance is increased so that health boards may meet up to 100 per cent of the revenue costs of projects for up to three years. Tapering begins after this period although the precise pattern is for local decision. The normal limit for payments through support finance is seven years. In exceptional cases, not specified in the circular, support finance may be extended for a maximum of 13 years.

Somewhat ironically, therefore, in the light of the PAC's concern that joint/support finance was not under adequate control given its increasing size and importance, the Scottish Office has decided quite consciously and deliberately to move towards a system where it has *less* control over events. The new system has given rise to some anxiety on the part of a number of health boards. Those boards which did well out of the previous bidding system will no longer do so since their indicative allocations involve smaller sums. The new system is likely, too, to have a constraining effect on the type and scale of development for which support finance is sought.

The SHHD is committed to reviewing the changes introduced by the 1985 circular after a year or so. Further adjustments may flow from this assessment, although it is extremely unlikely that there will be a return to greater central intervention.

While in many respects arrangements in Scotland for the use of support finance closely resemble those in England for joint finance there is an important exception. Whereas the DHSS allows health authorities to use centrally-earmarked joint finance up to a maximum of 13 years (ten years at 100 per cent) to meet the transitional costs incurred in transferring patients from hospital to community care, this facility is not available in Scotland. Whereas the DHSS puts additional sums into the joint finance pool to promote care in the community initiatives, the Scottish Office did not offer a similar facility because it wished to discontinue the use of centrally-earmarked finance and did not want to complicate arrangements by offering additional finance to meet the transitional costs of similar projects in Scotland. In the view of the Scottish Office, such problems ought to be settled locally.

FINANCIAL INCENTIVES FOR COMMUNITY CARE: WALES

Origins and objectives

In keeping with thinking in England and Scotland, joint finance in Wales was seen as desirable to 'encourage and facilitate joint planning' (Welsh Office 1977, paragraph 13, page 4) and 'to ease the constraints which arise from the necessary dividing line between two separately accountable services' (paragraph 9, page 3) . However, the circular emphasised that 'the major task is to make a reality of joint planning, most of which will not involve the use of joint finance' (paragraph 13, 4). Indeed, joint finance was introduced a year later than in England following a long argument within Wales at all levels as to whether it should be introduced at all. A Welsh Office official said there

> ... is a respectable argument that joint finance is a confusion. That when you've got separate authorities, separately constituted by Parliament with their expenditure separately voted, you shouldn't be confusing their roles in that way. That if county councils think that social services have priority they will develop them.

In Wales there was greater scepticism over the alleged benefits of joint

148

finance for joint planning and, consequently, a different emphasis from that evident in England. Whereas the DHSS defined the principal purpose of joint finance as being to promote joint planning, in Wales, as an official put it, 'we've tended to think of it more in terms of a mechanism to develop services'. Possibly this scepticism accounts for differences between the two countries governing the use of joint finance. Whilst in respect of 'care in the community' projects more flexibility is possible, in most other cases the local authority is expected to contribute 40 per cent of the total and the Welsh Office then provides half the health authority's contribution of 60 per cent. However, there is some flexibility in arriving at the permutation of tapering arrangements which best suits the needs of individual authorities under circumstances prevailing at any given time. But, as the Health Advisory Service (HAS) has argued, 'this still does not provide the same incentive for authorities to plan together as does the English system which (by top-slicing at national level) provides sums in the order of £300,000/£400,000 to the average health authority' (Health Advisory Service and Social Work Service of the Welsh Office 1985a, paragraph 27, page 5). We comment further on the operation of joint finance in the next subsection.

The amounts available for joint finance in Wales were relatively small compared with England but between 1980/81 and 1982/83 were the same as Scotland on a *per capita* basis (see Table 7). Thereafter, spending in Wales was considerably more modest than in Scotland and fell in absolute terms in 1985/86. However, further additional sums were beginning to be invested in the All Wales Strategy by that date. Nonetheless, underbidding for joint finance meant there was no question ever of turning anybody down. 'Any decent joint finance scheme would get funded' in the words of one official. Possibly, as in Scotland, poor take-up was a factor in the amounts available for joint finance remaining low.

The development of joint finance

The key features of the Welsh scheme are set out in columns 5 and 6 in Table 8. After its first year of operation, 1977, the Welsh system of joint finance resembled that which operated in Scotland from 1980 to 1985. Joint finance is earmarked centrally by top-slicing from the NHS vote and bids are invited for contributions from this pool. However, in contrast to England, and to Scotland prior to 1985, it is only the central government portion that is top-sliced. Health authorities are normally expected to fund 50 per cent of the total NHS contributions from their general allocations. As the Permanent Secretary at the Welsh Office told the PAC in January 1983:

149

We in the Welsh Office then scruntinise bids and approve the phasing of payments in respect of each individual project. This means that we do clearly from the centre have rather more control in Wales than exists in the English system . . . (paragraph 478, page 5).

The reasons for this arrangement have already been described in the earlier section on Scotland.

For a brief time – from June 1977 when the first circular on joint finance appeared until April 1978 when it was superseded by a second circular – the Welsh Office ruled out a central reserve bidding system on the grounds that it 'would necessitate reducing the finance available for general distribution' among health authorities (Welsh Office 1977, paragraph 12, page 4). Health authorities had let it be known that, 'at a time when all areas face severe constraints, funding of a development in one area should not be carried out through reductions of resources in others'. A central reserve would distort local priorities and decisions on the best use of resources. Accordingly, the Secretary of State decided that a health authority's contributions to agreed schemes should be met from its normal allocation.

However, the arrangement was short-lived. In 1978 a further circular announced that the situation had changed (Welsh Office 1978). 'The Secretary of State has recently been able to make an additional £1 million available to the Health Services out of which a central reserve of £0.2 million has been created for assistance to jointly financed projects in 1978/79' (paragraph 1, page 1). Unlike England and Scotland, then, joint finance in its second year of operation did, in a sense, involve additional 'new' money rather than merely top-slicing from the overall NHS allocation. A 1979 circular on the size of the central reserve stated that 'for planning purposes authorities may assume that it will consist entirely of new money' (Welsh Office 1979, paragraph 1, page 1).

The Welsh Office adopted a central bidding system in order to permit certain types of development to proceed which would have been difficult to support if the pool had been allocated to health authorities on a *pro rata* basis. With some reluctance because, according to an official, 'it's a huge chore on very limited resources', the bidding system was introduced. The development and operation of the bidding system is in marked contrast to events in Scotland. A deliberate decision to concentrate resources centrally was taken in Wales in order to support particular proposals which some authorities had put forward. Moreover, the Welsh Office was not convinced that every authority could make good use of the money and that a selective approach had some advantages.

In 1983, following a period of consultation on the *Care in the Community* document (Welsh Office 1981), which listed various options intended to provide incentives to aid joint planning, revised arrangements for joint finance were contained in a circular (Welsh Office 1983b). The changes brought Wales more into line with arrangements in England. The maximum period of joint finance for schemes aimed at enabling people to move out of hospital was ten years at 100 per cent funding and 13 years of joint funding in all. The scope of joint finance was also extended to housing and education. Special arrangements, already described in Chapter 5, applied to the development of mental handicap services and were additional to any initiatives receiving support from joint finance.

Although Ministers considered relaxing the rules on joint finance to allow 100 per cent funding for ten years with tapering over a further five they declined to do so except in respect of moving people out of hospital as mentioned above. Ministers concluded that the claim that the requirement normally placed on health authorities to fund 50 per cent of the NHS contribution to jointly financed schemes was a disincentive remained unproven. Underbidding for funds in the early years had given way to a situation in 1982/83 where, in contrast to Scotland, bidding exceeded by several times the amount available. Moreover, the 50 per cent rule was administered flexibly in order that higher contributions from the centre might be made available in exceptional circumstances. This assessment of the position is challenged by some officials who claim that underbidding remains a serious problem and that part of the explanation for this lies in the rules governing the use of joint finance. One official suggested that the fact that health authorities have to find a contribution for PSS schemes out of their own discretionary allocation 'might possibly be one of the reasons which explains this very distinctive pattern of underbidding'. In hard times the disincentive effect of this rule is even greater. Officials believe that if the major inhibiting factor is the requirement placed upon health authorities to find a discretionary contribution then the Welsh Office 'could do more by altering the rules'. On the other hand 'if, as most of the health people in the Welsh Office believe, it is actually local authority reluctance to pick up the tab at the end of the day, then our tarting around with the rules won't make any difference'.

It is the practice in Wales for proposals for joint finance to be initiated within the JCC by either the local or the health authority, or to originate from within the JCPT. Joint finance has been used to support projects of benefit to elderly, mentally handicapped and mentally ill people. In contrast to Scotland, mentally ill people have done particularly well out of joint finance (see Table 10). Use of joint finance is uneven. Five local authorities use it, three do not.

Table 10 Joint finance allocations: all Wales summary

	Totals *1978/79–1982/83**	*% of all Wales* *allocations*
Mental Illness	874,174	34.5
Mental Handicap	1,139,602	45.0
Elderly	339,859	13.4
Other	176,504	7.0

*At 1982 price levels.

Source: Welsh Office Joint Finance Analysis. Prepared for Public Accounts
Committee 1983. Joint Finance Key Figures – Sheet 2(A)

Welsh Office officials were sufficiently concerned at the problems surrounding joint finance to mount a review of the mechanism. However, the outcome is not known at the time of writing. Clearly there is disagreement in the Welsh Office over what constitutes the disincentive effect of joint finance – the rules governing the scheme, or the requirement for local authorities to pick up the tab after seven years. There is, however, agreement that joint finance is not working as effectively as it should.

Other financial incentives

There are other mechanisms besides joint finance in Wales to ensure the transfer of resources from hospital to community services. A reordering of priorities within the public expenditure survey in favour of PSS means that provision in local authority spending is higher than actual spending. As a Welsh Office official argued, 'nobody can accuse us of not making the provision on the resources side to have this anticipated shift. Maybe more needs to be done [but] hopefully the financial arrangements will deliver the reality'. Whereas the tapering arrangements for joint finance make some local authorities wary about entering into such schemes, the mental handicap strategy and its funding offer a more attractive incentive. An official explained: 'there is a promise that at the end of the Strategy period the resources will be permanently made available via the rate support grant, so the authorities are much happier over that kind of arrangement.

The need for bridging finance to enable new developments to start up before closing existing facilities was accepted. Also, according to an official:

... you need a mechanism to be able to make it (ie the money) over which doesn't give health authorities or any other party a veto. That seems to me a fundamental weakness of joint finance ... people have tended to confuse joint planning with joint control or joint management.

The various initiatives launched by the Welsh Office have brought additional money to social services departments to the extent that, according to the HAS, 'planning with the Welsh Office has come to assume more significance (in scale) than joint planning between health and social services authorities (Health Advisory Service and Social Work Service of the Welsh Office 1985a, paragraph 28, page 5). One official argued that none of the mechanisms would be necessary if there was a proper planning system *in situ*. 'All these things are a substitute .. it's belt, braces and a piece of string. Until we have the confidence that the new planning system is operating well I don't think ministers will drop these special ways of doing things.'

SUMMARY

Our review of financial incentives to promote joint planning has revealed sharp differences in aspects of their purpose and design. Three in particular merit comment:

1   the conception of joint/support finance as primarily a pool of pump priming, or seed, money to stimulate joint developments (as in Scotland and Wales), or as a means of encouraging joint planning (as in England);

2   the choice between bidding arrangements for joint/support finance (as in Scotland, from 1980 to 1985, and Wales) and their allocation to health authorities according to a formula (as in England);

3   (linked to 2) the varying arrangements for targeting and controlling joint/support finance in each of the three countries.

There are also some general problems associated with joint/support finance which are common to the three countries and we conclude with these.

From the start in Wales and Scotland joint/support finance enjoyed a lower profile than in England. Not only was it introduced later but the amounts involved were substantially smaller and have remained so. Although each of the countries saw the mechanism as a stimulus to joint planning, the connection was most pronounced in England. In Wales and Scotland, there was a great emphasis on joint/support finance as a means of initiating new developments on an experimental basis. This difference in approach appears to be reflected in the more generous and flexible arrangements governing the use of joint finance in England. Much of the increased flexibility benefited local authorities which may be indicative of a greater influence on the part of the local authority associations. Significantly, much of the pressure for following the DHSS lead in Scotland has come from outside pressure groups rather than from the Convention of Scottish Local Authorities (COSLA). It is worth noting Keating and Midwinter's (1983, page 107) claim that unlike the English local authority associations, 'COSLA is not well geared up to influencing Parliamentary legislation'. Although COSLA is unique in representing all the various local authorities, a united front is rarely achieved because authorities' interests do not always coincide (Craig 1980). COSLA's weakness is therefore a consequence of its alleged strength. There was also in Scotland a reluctance to introduce support finance at all since earmarking has never been an instrument favoured by the Scottish Office, primarily because it ran counter to its underlying preference for a 'hands off' delegated approach to management and control as we pointed out in Chapter 3.

A central bidding arrangement for joint/support finance has operated in Wales from the second year of the scheme's operation and in Scotland for the first four years. Compared with the English system this has both strengths and limitations. On the one hand, it provides the centre with a more direct means of securing accountability for the expenditure of NHS resources on local authority services. Similarly, it enhances the capacity of government departments to target resources on particular authorities and also on schemes which are clearly supportive of NHS objectives. As we have noted, both these features have been identified as problematic in the English context not least by the Public Accounts Committee (PAC). However, not too much should be made of this distinction. Central departments have not attempted to appraise or evaluate the contribution of joint/support finance to improving health care even when, as in the case of the Welsh Office or the SHHD, the central department has been directly involved in assessing bids put up by health authorities. This oversight led to some concern on the part of the PAC which was anxious to ensure not simply that procedures for the control and accountability of this pool of money were adequate but that evidence of their effectiveness in achieving their stated purpose would be forthcoming. The PAC was sceptical that joint/support finance represented value for money or was desirable in the long term.

On the other hand, the English system of allocating joint finance has the advantage of promoting at least a minimal degree of interaction between every health authority and its related local authorities. Under the English scheme, local agencies cannot opt out of the process of agreeing a joint finance programme. In Scotland and Wales a number

154

of localities have refused to participate in the scheme. Given the more limited sums available in Scotland and Wales, this is not entirely a disadvantage in that the funds have been spread less thinly thereby enabling more sizeable projects to be supported. At the same time, however, the central bidding system means that the opportunities for all authorities in England to learn about inter-agency cooperation are not applicable to Scotland or Wales. And it is in Scotland and Wales that these opportunities are most needed because of the historically low level of inter-authority contact. As we noted earlier, the Health Advisory Service (Health Advisory Service and Social Work Service of the Welsh Office 1985a) has argued this point in relation to Wales believing that the system of joint finance may have inhibited the level of joint planning between health and social services authorities.

Although it is too early to pass final judgement on the post-1985 arrangements for allocating support finance in Scotland, available evidence suggests that neither the advantages of a bidding system nor of a system along the lines of the English model will be forthcoming. The system of indicative allocations is subsumed within total health authority budgets and support finance is thus less securely insulated from pressures to spend the resources on health services, including the acute sector. The English experience (that is, the doubling of DHA spending of joint finance on community health services) suggests that even when resources are earmarked the NHS will still seek to deploy them on its own services. The position in Scotland, then, seems to represent the worst of all possible worlds.

More generally, as we have shown, although it has to some extent served as a spur to collaboration and joint planning, the mechanism of joint/support finance has not been devoid of difficulties and drawbacks across the three countries. Four in particular stand out.

First, because the amount of joint/support finance to any health authority is limited there are built-in restrictions on the type and scale of project that can be supported.

Secondly, joint/support finance is designed to taper off at some point until the funding is taken over by the participating local authority. Successive resource squeezes on local government have created additional difficulties in decisions over whether or not to use joint/support finance because of concern that, in the longer-term, it may not be possible to sustain developments which have been given life through this pump priming mechanism. In a turbulent financial and economic environment, joint/support finance is a double-edged weapon. Moreover, the temptation increasingly is to use this ready source of funds to make up for cuts in main budgets and to shore up services which may have suffered from present policies. Schemes have been put forward which in bygone days would probably have been funded from main budgets rather than from joint/support finance.

Thirdly, it is not always easy to distinguish between schemes which are in the interests of the NHS, and therefore could be expected to make a better contribution to total care than if the funds were directly applied to health services, and those which are clearly of less direct relevance to the NHS or to health status. The difficulty is that most social services' activity involving any of the priority client groups is likely to have implications of one sort or another for health services. Most schemes put forward for support have been instigated by local authorities and, with few exceptions, health authorities in general have not sought to evaluate the projects funded from joint/support finance or rigorously to assess their expected benefits to the NHS.

Finally, the state of affairs we have depicted at local level is a dramatic reflection of the absence of a joint approach to policy within central government departments and illustrates how one department's policy output can impinge upon, and possibly distort or contradict, that of another department (Royal Institute of Public Administration 1981). In many fields of policy, as we suggested in Chapter 2, central departments in each of the three countries appear to work against rather than with each other.

Chapter 8
CONCLUSION

How far does the case of community care support the twin notions that policy uniformity prevails in a unitary state and that the Whitehall departments take the lead in determining the basic shape and direction of national policies? At one level, we have found some support for this view: community care has been advocated in the major policy documents issued by each of the health departments over at least the last decade. Equally, the DHSS can be seen to have set both the tone and framework for policy debate in this area from which the Scottish and Welsh Offices subsequently took their cues. The initial review of mental handicap policy was conducted by the DHSS (which was still responsible for health and personal social services in Wales when the exercise commenced) and its fundamental service principles were included, without change, in the subsequent Scottish document. More recently, the DHSS lead on joint finance and resource transfers has been followed by similar initiatives in Scotland and Wales, although in both cases there are detailed differences between these and the DHSS arrangements.

Yet it is equally clear from our study that this is by no means the whole picture. Our assessment of how each of the three countries has responded, and is responding, to the community care strategy at national level, both generally and with regard to mental handicap services in particular, has identified substantive policy as well as organisational differences between, and also within, each of the countries. The Scottish Office has never pursued community care with anything like the degree of enthusiasm and conviction shown by the DHSS and the Welsh Office. Our review of expenditure and service patterns in Chapter 4 demonstrated the marked bias towards hospital provision in Scotland. At the same time, the Welsh mental handicap initiative represents a radical departure from the common policy framework within which England and Wales operated during the 1970s. It is true that at a general level, the commitment to community care is to be found in official documents relating to all three countries. To this extent, the rhetoric has probably been picked up from the DHSS but it would be greatly over-simplifying reality to conclude that the DHSS has therefore given a policy *lead* to Wales and Scotland. Since both countries have proceeded in quite opposite directions from one another and display major differences from

England, the evidence points to a substantial degree of independent policy-determination within a general but flexible framework. As our discussion of mental handicap policy in Chapter 5 underlined, there are now substantial divergences between England, Scotland and Wales, not simply in the pace of implementation but also in the fundamental goals, values and outputs associated with community care. To a very considerable extent, policies for mentally handicapped people appear as the products of three independent nations rather than as modest differences readily accommodated within a unitary structure of policy objectives.

The explanation of such differences is not straightforward and could be firmly established only by study of both a more extensive and intensive nature than our resources allowed. There are some pointers but we should be cautious in ascribing causal relationships between different factors. There are, for example, some associations between organisational structures, financial arrangements and policy outputs, as we discuss below. However, the impact of historical, cultural, environmental and ideological influences on policy outputs should not be overlooked. It could be that the rather more fragmented, departmental arrangements in the Scottish Office, which militate against close working relationships across service boundaries, may themselves reflect the lower priority attached to such activity. Equally, the key financial mechanism in Wales for directing health resources into social services development was devised precisely because a particular philosophy of care was so highly valued. The Welsh mental handicap strategy clearly demonstrates the capacity of a determined Secretary of State in a territorial department to cut across functional boundaries and shift resources between services in ways not open to his English counterpart, particularly the utilisation of the discretionary powers devolved in the early 1980s. Less clear is the influence of such political and administrative factors in the initiation of policy: how far they allowed the Welsh Office to think what in the English or Scottish context would have been unthinkable, albeit for different reasons, and how far they merely allowed it to run with a policy once it had been formulated. It seems unlikely, however, that means do not play a role in the determination of ends, as well as *vice versa*. Mechanisms for policy and financial integration are normally established precisely in order to generate, as well as implement, policy options which span service boundaries. Where they do not have an initiatory role, they may at least maintain such options on an active policy agenda.

Even so, such instruments need to be seen alongside the contribution of perhaps more fundamental forces associated with the distribution of power and influence. For example, as the DHSS response to the Jay committee illustrated, the entrenched interests of the medical and nursing professions in England have kept radical approaches, similar to the All Wales Strategy, off national (but, interestingly, not all local – see North Western Regional Health Authority 1982) policy agendas despite the presence of integrative structures for policy-making within the Department. Indeed, it is at least arguable that in reflecting the balance of power and interests inherent in existing services, the composition of client group planning teams in the DHSS ensures that only modest shifts in policy take place, leaving the *status quo* relatively undisturbed. In particular, the minority and, in some respects, marginal nature of the role played by the Social Services Inspectorate in DHSS policy-making contrasts strikingly with the leading role social services departments would be asked to play at local level if more radical models of community care were to be implemented. As the Welsh Office initially found, a policy-making process dominated by medical/nursing interests tends to reproduce service models in which medical/nursing interests and perspectives predominate (see Chapter 5). It was only when the policy process was opened up to a wider range of interests that an alternative service model became the basis of the All Wales Strategy.

Similar considerations appear to apply, but more forcefully, to Scotland where the organisational arrangements for integrated planning are much weaker than in the DHSS and where the predominant medical preference for institutional forms of care is, if anything, even more influential than in England. In Scotland the notion of community care does not sit easily alongside the traditional concepts of care which largely determine health policy and which are widely held by sections of the medical profession and other professions. At all levels, political, administrative and professional, a more hospital-oriented perspective has been the dominant influence and there has been no sustained attempt to challenge it. In part this may be because the relatively high numbers of beds and other health resources has minimised cost-push and demand-pull pressures for the development of alternatives to hospital provision, especially for the elderly. Yet the continued reliance on relatively large-scale hospital provision for mental illness and mental handicap suggests the influence of additional factors located in the wider professional and social culture. Pressure for change is weak and comes mainly from interest groups and 'issue networks' operating outside the NHS of which the Care in the Community Scottish Working Group representing 22 voluntary bodies has been the most influential example. As in England, the influence of such lobbies and networks ought not to be discounted in the formation of policy (Haywood and Hunter 1982). Also, it is conceivable that, were services under greater pressure in resource terms, this would have provided the trigger for a wider debate about community care as seems to have been the case, at least in part, in England. As it is, Scotland's markedly different infrastructure of services, with its greater proportion of hospital beds, means that pressure for change would have to be very much stronger than hitherto if the forces for maintaining the *status quo* were to be overcome.

We have argued that the field of community care is marked by policy diversity rather than policy uniformity. This is not to imply, however, that forces acting in the contrary direction do not exist. First, we would acknowledge that strong pressures for the alignment of policy exist within Britain and not least as a result of pressure group activity. At the end of the day, the Scottish Office would almost certainly not have introduced the original support finance scheme nor the resource transfer/care in the community arrangements, albeit much more limited in scope than in England, had not the DHSS taken the lead and the professional lobbies within Scotland argued for their extension to Scotland (the 'me too' factor at work as one official put it). However, those pressures for policy alignment do not operate in one direction alone; they apply to the DHSS as well. The Welsh example – particularly in its commitment of new resources to fund community care – may increasingly be taken up by interest groups in England as a model which the DHSS should follow. A second factor militating against policy divergence is the relative lack of policy-making resources in Edinburgh and, most particularly, Cardiff compared with London. For example, the Welsh Office would have been hard put to establish a study group on community care equivalent to the DHSS one. If for no other reason, this factor is an important constraint on the extent to which the Scottish and Welsh Offices are able to initiate independent policy stances *de novo* and across as broad a canvas as the DHSS. In these circumstances a selective approach is dictated. One of the most interesting findings of our study is the extent to which this approach has been consciously adopted, particularly in the Welsh Office where an official described the tactic of fishing 'with a wide-meshed net so that we always caught the big important fish (in our terms) while the tiddlers were consciously allowed to get away'.

Potentially of more significance, however, is the growth of self-confidence in Edinburgh, but more especially (and recently) in Cardiff, which suggests that policy divergence may become more frequent in future. Neither of the territorial departments, for example, felt obliged to follow the lead set by the DHSS in producing the priorities handbook, *Care in Action*, despite its strong associations with the political philosophy of the Thatcher administration. The Welsh Office felt able to ignore the exercise altogether while Scotland

160

had already gone its own way in producing *SHAPE*, which was much more in keeping with the allegedly dirigiste traditions of the 1970s and to which, in England, *Care in Action* was explicitly a reaction. In the case of the Griffiths reforms, the two territorial departments followed the DHSS example, though with markedly less enthusiasm in Scotland than in Wales. Indeed, it was only political enthusiasm at the highest level in Whitehall that ensured the introduction of general management in Scotland. Nevertheless, as we indicated in Chapter 4, the spirit of Griffiths is in danger of being diluted if the guidance on senior management structures is anything to judge by. In this case, and even more so with Scottish Office policies towards community care, differences in policy means may effectively conceal more deep-rooted differences in support for fundamental policy objectives. They may also be indicative of a weaker political input into the policy process.

We quoted in an earlier chapter the contrary view of a Scottish Office official who suggested it was the *way* things were done rather than the *things* themselves that was different and distinctive. Two policy initiatives which may appear to agree with this view are the 1982–85 structural and managerial changes in the NHS across Britain, and the long-standing commitment to community care and joint planning. But the administrative and professional means by which such policy ends have been, or are being, sought differ so considerably that the policy stances themselves have become, or are becoming, subtly modified and redefined. Our analysis of the policy context surrounding community care in Chapter 4 demonstrated this process at work to a greater degree even than was apparent in respect of the structural and managerial changes in the NHS described in Chapter 2. Indeed, were it not for sustained pressure from interest groups within Scotland for the SHHD to ape English practice, or at any rate components of it, then policy deviation might have been even more pronounced. The Scottish Office has a preference, as others have also noted (Parry 1985), for a 'hands-off' approach to government and a consequent lack of means to steer rather than react to policy. A contributing factor may be the weaker political input already mentioned. Perhaps more evident in Scotland than in Wales is the fact that administration is very largely left to take care of itself. As we noted in Chapter 2, Scottish Office ministers spend a considerable amount of time at Westminster when Parliament is meeting. The existence of a substantial degree of administrative devolution in Edinburgh alongside political centralisation at Westminster may contribute to the particular policy environment and style of operating which we have described in Scotland.

Certainly, the strength of political commitment to the ends and means of community care appears to have been a key influence at critical points in the evolution of community care in both England and Wales. As the first Secretary of State for Social Services, and especially after the Ely Hospital scandal, Richard Crossman was the principal driving force behind policies to improve the status of 'Cinderella' client groups. Subsequently, Barbara Castle and David Owen were particularly influential in the introduction of joint finance in 1976 and the accompanying framework for joint planning, with its more prescriptive flavour than the equivalent developments in Scotland and Wales. At that time, in marked contrast, ministerial commitment was less apparent in Wales where joint finance was not introduced until the following year, and then at a significantly lower *per capita* level. Similarly, guidance on the establishment of joint planning was more general. It was only when the Welsh Secretary threw his weight behind the development of community care for mentally handicapped people that well-developed planning and financial mechanisms were devised to achieve this end (see Chapter 5). In Scotland, the relative dearth of joint planning reflects weaker guidance from the centre as is evidenced by the absence of a statutory requirement to establish joint planning machinery. Moreover, while it may have to concede defeat, the Scottish Office is resisting pressure to replace the voluntary arrangement with a directive on planning machinery. The later introduction of support finance and the more recent shift to a system based on indicative allocations (see Chapter 7) similarly demonstrate a weakness of means consistent with a policy context in which community care is accorded relatively lower priority. Speeches by the former Health Minister, John MacKay, and his successor, Lord Glenarthur, do not suggest an unequivocal political commitment to community care in Scotland similar to that in England and Wales.

The significance of joint planning and joint finance is that they are the key instruments by which community care might become a reality at local level. At first sight the variations between these instruments in the three countries seem to be consistent with the view that the territorial departments are free to develop divergent means within a unitary policy framework. However, this would be a misleading and over-simplistic conclusion to draw from our study. As we have demonstrated, these differences in means reflect differences in the weight accorded to the underlying policy objective of community care. In this sense, it is the congruence between the means and the ends which each country has chosen to adopt that reflects the capacity of each health department to devise divergent approaches to policy rather than merely distinctive mechanisms for achieving identical ends.

There are, of course, other ways in which means and ends are

162

interdependent, and they are certainly much less easy to separate out than is implied by the suggestion that diversity in policy-making is possible only in so far as it encompasses variations in the implementation of policies made elsewhere. Indeed, as we stated in Chapter 1, the linear model of the policy process on which such views are implicitly founded is now widely accepted to be over-simplistic, if not naive. Policy implementers are themselves likely to make policy, particularly in those situations where there are multiple objectives, where the policy in question is not of the highest priority to those at higher levels, and where considerable discretion is a feature of the work. Such influences are in evidence in community care policy both *within* each of the three countries comprising Britain and *between* them, although we would not wish to imply that London is the sole policy-making level while Edinburgh and Cardiff merely implement policy that is handed down. Our approach, *inter alia*, has been to challenge such a view. At the same time, as we argue below, the DHSS may be said to give a lead of sorts on occasion which the Scottish and Welsh Offices can choose to follow or ignore.

Our study suggests, therefore, that the territorial departments not only have greater opportunities to choose to act independently of Whitehall than has normally been suggested hitherto but that their endorsement of apparently similar policies may be in such broad terms, or the implementation process so different, that the degree of uniformity in policy-making is very substantially less than it might seem at first sight. All of this points to the need for caution in allowing similarities in the policy lexicon to cloak real differences in policy meaning, intent and practice.

Our study indicates that the nature of the relationship between London, Edinburgh and Cardiff is altogether more complex than is often assumed. The behaviour of the territorial departments suggests that, in practice, as well as in principle, a number of quite different strategies may be open to them, particularly where, as in the health and personal social services field, their policy-making capacity is high (Parry 1985). Thus the Scottish and Welsh Offices may:

1   follow the DHSS lead, enthusiastically but with minor adaptations to local circumstances (for example, the implementation of Griffiths in Wales);

2   follow the DHSS lead unenthusiastically, that is, in the most general and symbolic of terms and with the most limited follow-through so that policy outputs vary substantially across Britain even though policy goals display a semblance of uniformity (for example, in Scotland, community care, joint planning, and the revised support finance scheme);

3 ignore the DHSS lead and do something different (for example, *SHAPE* in Scotland; the All Wales Strategy);

4 ignore the DHSS lead and do nothing (for example, no equivalent of *Care in Action* in Wales, of joint finance in Scotland until 1980, or of the *Care in the Community* consultative document in Scotland).

At the same time, we should beware of interpreting events as if the DHSS were always the lead department with the traffic flowing all one way. The fact that the DHSS most often assumes a lead role is a consequence of its more substantial resources and greater capacity for policy exploration and development. In this sense the lead role becomes one of demonstrating what is possible by example. However, in mental handicap policy, for instance, Wales may, in time, prove to have exercised the lead Department role. This has already proved to be true of Scotland in respect of the creation of the English Mental Health Act Commission in 1984, where the DHSS followed an earlier Scottish Office example – the Mental Welfare Commission set up in 1960. Barring any unforeseeable technical problems, Scottish rating reform – the replacement of local rates with a community charge – will take place in advance of that in England or Wales. Moreover, various changes in local government finance, in police powers, and in juvenile justice have been pioneered in Scotland, with England, in all but the last case, following at a later date.

On the other hand, if there appear to be opportunities for territorial departments to determine whether and, if so, in what ways to follow the DHSS lead, we should not overlook the fundamental parameters imposed by a unitary political system. It is inconceivable, for example, that one or both of the territorial departments could independently introduce charges for health care. It is also highly improbable that the amalgamation of health and personal social services could be introduced in Wales or Scotland, if only because the interest groups in England would speedily mobilise to resist what they would undoubtedly see as the 'thin end of the wedge'.

Beyond such fundamental issues it is difficult to be categoric about the limits to policy divergence if only because the situation is a developing one. We have already encountered somewhat greater variations than might have been predicted and it will be important to monitor the extent to which the health and personal social services are atypical of public policy as a whole. It may be that the degree of policy autonomy within the Welsh and Scottish Offices varies considerably according to the particular policy field or even issues within it. A useful notion here is Bulpitt's (1983) distinction between the 'low politics' of the periphery and the 'high politics' of the core. Unless the policy area is of crucial political and managerial importance to the core then it is likely that territorial variations will be tolerated if not encouraged. In other words, if a policy field falls within the category of 'low politics' then the space for policy-making at the periphery is likely to be more substantial, and *vice versa*.

In some fields of policy some of the strategies outlined above may not be open to the Scottish and Welsh Offices because their independent influence is that much more circumscribed. The most obvious potential examples here lie in the field of economic affairs where the context is largely set by national policies and it is difficult, if not impossible, for Scotland and Wales to swim entirely against the tide. The closure of the Gartcosh rolling mill provides an example, although the retention of the Ravenscraig steel works would suggest that even here the Scottish Office may not be uninfluential in modifying national policies but perhaps only in the short term. Indeed, in many respects government intervention in the Scottish and Welsh economies as exemplified, for example, by the work of the Development Agencies, is more akin to the Wilsonian politics of the 1960s than to the Thatcherite politics of the 1980s and is certainly more evident than in England. At the same time, it should be emphasised that the scope for autonomy in policy-making is limited by Treasury control of total public expenditure. While the Scottish and Welsh Secretaries can, if they so wish, shift resources around within their programmes, historical commitments combined with very restricted growth increments not only limit such changes to the margin, but also limit the number of occasions on which independent initiatives can be taken where these have additional spending consequences. Nonetheless, we would not exclude the possibility that detailed studies of individual policy areas would reveal less policy uniformity outside, as well as within, the health and personal social services policy field than has hitherto been appreciated.

As a policy priority with scope for creativity in implementation, community care has provided an opportunity to test the notion of policy uniformity, the underlying reasons for differences in this field and, in particular, whether these are related to variations in policy ends, administrative means, or both. On the basis of our evidence we can only conclude that, contrary to the conventional wisdom, both are at play. But does our study have any practical lessons which go beyond such niceties of academic inquiry? At least three such lessons may be identified.

First, our study suggests the limited importance of structure in determining policy outputs. On the one hand, structural fragmentation at the centre in Scotland serves as a barrier to the development of an integrated and coherent community care policy compared with the more unified structures within which health and personal social

165

services policy-making takes place in the DHSS and the Welsh Office. At the same time, the Welsh Office as a single department with responsibility for both service development and resource allocation has been able to move further towards implementation of a community care policy for mentally handicapped people than has generally been possible in England where such responsibilities are divided between the DHSS, the DoE and the Treasury. In these respects, therefore, structural factors appear to have been important in facilitating policy outcomes. On the other hand, structural configurations are in themselves a reflection of more pervasive and underlying process factors. For example, the DHSS client group structure reflects a commitment to unified policy-making across health and personal social services which is, in large measure, based upon a prior commitment to promote community care and the interests of dependency groups. In Scotland, where the key professional interests and values appear less oriented towards community care, it should be seen as no accident that structural arrangements (or their absence) reflect such an orientation.

Second, following on from the above considerations, a narrow belief that getting the structure right will in itself lead to successful policy outcomes is misconceived. The indisputable need for appropriate enabling structures should not be allowed to obscure the prior, and ultimately more important, need to be clear about the purpose such structures are intended to serve. The tendency at local level for planners to devote more attention to the fine detail of collaborative mechanisms rather than to the often more contentious questions concerning desired service patterns is an example of this deficiency. Policy clarity needs to be the engine to drive joint planning. In this context, the focus in *Progress in Partnership* (Working Group on Joint Planning 1985) on a strengthened joint consultative committee as the engine for joint planning could be seen as making the mistake of putting structure first. There are fundamental questions about the allocation of service responsibilities and models of care which ought not to be left in a vacuum by central government any more than by local policy-makers. One of the lessons from the All Wales Strategy is precisely the overriding importance of clarifying policy objectives in the first instance and of only subsequently devising financial and planning arrangements which comprise, and reinforce, a total strategy. Similar considerations need to apply at local level if local actors are not to be seduced into believing that structure is a substitute for purpose. Those interests seeking change in the current pattern of policy outputs should be no less concerned to avoid an over-concentration on structural apparatus. It offers no panacea.

Third, and more prosaically, this review of community care policy in Britain and its various manifestations affords an opportunity for policy learning. There has, for example, been more experience of joint planning in England than in either Scotland or Wales. In principle, therefore, this affords the opportunity for the latter two countries to short-circuit potential difficulties in this field by learning from events in England. A recent flurry of interest in joint planning and community care in, for example, the Lothian, Grampian and Strathclyde regions suggests that the situation in Scotland may be beginning to change. If the opportunity is taken to avoid some of the pitfalls of the earlier English experience, progress could be correspondingly more rapid. Another area for policy learning was identified in Chapters 4 and 5 where we noted different models of care and service mixes in the three countries whose costs and benefits remain unexplored. In a situation where there is no right answer or one best way, the systematic evaluation of these variations seems appropriate.

Unlike most cross-national research, differences in culture and context, though real, are less pronounced in Britain. Attempts to take advantage of this situation might well repay investment (Hunter 1982 and 1983a; Wistow 1985). However it is not clear that the opportunities for policy learning and research within Britain have been fully grasped or that sufficiently well-developed networks exist for such learning to take place. This is unfortunate when our study of community care policy strongly suggests that there may be much of practical value to gain from intra-Britain comparisons.

REFERENCES

Allen D E (1982) Annual reviews or no annual reviews: the balance of power between the DHSS and health authorities. British Medical Journal, 285, 28 August–4 September: pp 665–667.

Arcade (1981) Mentally handicapped: Welsh Office's backward step. 20 February.

Baker N and Urquhart J (1986) The balance of care for mentally handicapped adults in Scotland. First report. Edinburgh, Information Services Division, Common Services Agency.

Beyer S, Evans G, Todd, S and Blunden R (1986) Planning for the all-Wales strategy: a review of issues arising in Welsh counties. Research report no 19. Cardiff, Mental Handicap in Wales Applied Research Unit.

Birch S and Maynard A (1986) Equalising access to health within the UK. Public Money, 6, 2, September: pp 54–55.

Birrell D and Williamson A (1983) Northern Ireland's integrated health and personal social service structure. In: Williamson A and Room G (eds) Health and welfare states of Britain: an inter-country comparison. London, Heinemann Educational: pp 130–150.

Blaxter M (1976) The meaning of disability. London, Heinemann.

Boddy D (1979) An experiment in the long-term planning of health care services. Public Administration, 57, Summer: pp 159–171.

Bonham-Carter M (1981) What's wrong with the Home Office. The Times, 16 January.

Booth T A (1979) Planning for welfare: social policy and the expenditure process. Oxford, Blackwell and Robertson.

Booth T A (1981) Collaboration between the health and social services: Part I – A case study of joint care planning. Policy and Politics, 9, 1: pp 23–49; Part II – A case study of joint finance. Policy and Politics, 9, 2: pp 205–226.

Brown R G S (1977) Accountability and control in the National Health Service. Health and Social Service Journal, Centre Eight Papers, 28 October: pp B9–B15.

Brown S (1985) Controversies and negotiations: a summary discussion of project policy. Aberdeen, University of Aberdeen (unpublished mimeo).

Bryant P (1985) A review of grant applications 1982–1985. Caerphilly, Opportunities for Volunteering in Wales.

168

Bulpitt J G (1983) Territory and power in the United Kingdom. Manchester, Manchester University Press.

Burns T (1981) Rediscovering organisation: aspects of collaboration and managerialism in hospital organisation. Edinburgh (unpublished mimeo).

Button J H (1984) Wales today. Hospital and Health Services Review, 80, 3, May: pp 110–115.

Butts M, Irving D and Whitt C (1981) From principles to practice: a commentary on health service planning and resource allocation in England from 1970 to 1980. London, Nuffield Provincial Hospitals Trust.

Care in the Community Scottish Working Group (1986a) Community care survey. Edinburgh.

Care in the Community Scottish Working Group (1986b) Report of a seminar for secretaries of joint liaison committees. 3 May, Glasgow.

Casper A (1985) A review of factors which influence the implementation of a policy of community care for elderly people with particular reference to Northern Ireland. Essay submitted to RIPA. Haldane Essay Competition, Cardiff (unpublished mimeo).

Castle B (1975) Speech to National Association of Health Authorities, 11 July.

Central Policy Review Staff (1977) Relations between central government and local authorities. London, HMSO.

Central Statistical Office (1986) Regional Trends 21. London, HMSO.

Cole P, McGuire A and Stuart P (1985) More money – better health care? A comparison of NHS spending and health service provision in Scotland and England. Discussion paper no 03/85. Aberdeen, Health Economics Research Unit, University of Aberdeen.

Connolly M (1985) Integrating health and social services: has the Northern Ireland experiment succeeded? Public Money, 4, 4, March: pp 25–28.

Cooper J (1983) The creation of the British personal social services 1962–74. London, Heinemann Educational.

Cotmore R, Sinclair R, Webb A and Wistow G (1985) Five faces of care. Community Care, 27 June: pp 15–18.

Craig C (1980) COSLA: a silent voice for local government? In: Drucker H M and Drucker N L (eds) The Scottish government yearbook 1981. Edinburgh, Paul Harris.

Davies P (1986a) Ex-maths teacher treads the boards. Health and Social Service Journal, 13 February: pp 204–205.

Davies P (1986b) Merifield keeps a low profile. The Health Service Journal, 28 August: pp 1130–1131.

Day P and Klein R (1983) The mobilisation of consent versus the management of conflict: decoding the Griffiths report. British Medical Journal, 287, 10 December: pp 1813–1816.

Day P and Klein R (1985a) Central accountability and local decision making: towards a new NHS. British Medical Journal, 290, 1 June: pp 1676–1678.

Day P and Klein R (1985b) Towards a new health care system? British Medical Journal, 291, 2 November: pp 1291–1293.

Department of Health and Social Security (1972a) Local authority social services ten year plans 1973–1983. Circular 35/72. London, DHSS.

Department of Health and Social Security (1972b) Management arrangements for the reorganised National Health Service. London, HMSO.

Department of Health and Social Security (1974) Collaboration between health and local authorities. Circular HRC(74) 19. London. DHSS.

Department of Health and Social Security (1975) Better services for the mentally ill. Cmnd 6233. London, HMSO.

Department of Health and Social Security (1976a) Joint care planning: health and local authorities. Circular HC(76) 18/LAC(76)6. London, DHSS.

Department of Health and Social Security (1976b) Priorities for health and personal social services in England: a consultative document. London, HMSO.

Department of Health and Social Security (1977a) Joint care planning: health and local authorities. Circular HC(77)17/LAC(77)10. London, DHSS.

Department of Health and Social Security (1977b) Priorities in the health and social services: the way forward. London, HMSO.

Department of Health and Social Security (1980) Mental handicap: progress, problems and priorities. London, DHSS.

Department of Health and Social Security (1981a) Care in action: a handbook of policies and priorities for the health and personal social services in England. London, HMSO.

Department of Health and Social Security (1981b) Care in the community: a consultative document on moving resources for care in England. London, DHSS.

Department of Health and Social Security (1981c) Report of a study on community care. London, DHSS.

Department of Health and Social Security (1983a) Health care and its costs: the development of the National Health Service in England. London, HMSO.

Department of Health and Social Security (1983b) Health service development: care in the community and joint finance. Circular HC(83)6/LAC(83)5. London, DHSS.

Department of Health and Social Security (1983c) NHS management inquiry. Report (Leader of inquiry, Roy Griffiths) London, DHSS.

Department of Health and Social Security (1983d) The social work service of the NHS: a consultative document. London, DHSS.

Department of Health and Social Security (1984) The health service in England. Annual report 1984. London, HMSO.

Department of Health and Social Security (1985a) Government response to the second report from the social services committee, 1984–85 session: community care. Cmnd 9674. London, HMSO.

Department of Health and Social Security (1985b) Supplementary benefit and residential care. Report of a joint central and local government working party. London, DHSS.

Department of Health and Social Security (1986) Collaboration between the NHS, local government and voluntary organisations: joint planning and collaboration. Draft circular, January. London, DHSS.

Department of Health and Social Security, Scottish Office, Welsh Office and Northern Ireland Office (1981) Growing older. Cmnd 8173. London. HMSO.

Department of Health and Social Security and Welsh Office (1971) Better services for the mentally handicapped. Cmnd 4683. London, HMSO.

Department of Health and Social Security and Welsh Office (1979) Patients first. Consultative paper on the structure and management of the NHS in England and Wales. London, HMSO.

Department of Health and Social Security and Welsh Office (1986) The function and management of the DHSS. Health Trends, 18, 2: pp 32–36.

Donges G (1982) Policymaking for the mentally handicapped. Aldershot, Gower.

Doyle M, Fuller S, Humble S, Mocroft I, Stubbings P, Webb A and Wistow G (1985) Opportunities for volunteering 1982–1985. Berkhamsted and Loughborough, Volunteer Centre/Centre for Research in Social Policy.

Drucker N (1986) Lost in the haar: a critique of mental health in focus. In: McCrone D (ed) The Scottish government yearbook 1986. Edinburgh, Unit for the Study of Government in Scotland: pp 70–92.

Elcock H and Haywood S (1980) The buck stops where?: accountability and control in the National Health Service. Hull, Institute for Health Studies, University of Hull.

Fowler N (1982) Speech to Age Concern, 11 May.

Gibson J S (1985a) Researching the Scottish Office: thoughts on 'the thistle and the crown'. Paper delivered at conference on the Scottish Office 1885–1985, 29–30 November. Edinburgh, University of Edinburgh.

171

Gibson J S (1985b) The thistle and the crown: a history of the Scottish Office. Edinburgh, HMSO.

Glennerster H with Korman N and Marslen-Wilson F (1983) Planning for priority groups. Oxford, Martin Robertston.

Goldsmith M (1986a) Managing the periphery in a period of fiscal stress. In: Goldsmith M (ed) (1986b) New research in central-local relations. Aldershot, Gower: pp 152–172.

Goldsmith M (ed) (1986b) New research in central-local relations. Aldershot, Gower.

Gray A M and Hunter D J (1983) Priorities and resource allocation in the Scottish health service: some problems in planning and implementation. Policy and Politics, II 4: pp 417–437.

Gray A M and Mooney, G H (1982) Health in Scotland. In: Cuthbert M (ed) Government spending in Scotland. Edinburgh, Paul Harris.

Griffiths J A G (1966) Central departments and local authorities. London, Allen and Unwin.

Gunn L (1976) New directions in public policy-making. A paper to the Scottish Health Service Planning Council. Edinburgh (unpublished mimeo).

Halpern S (1986a) Getting it right next time. The Health Service Journal, 10 July: pp 916–7.

Halpern S (1986b) Public convinced NHS is underfunded, reveals poll. The Health Service Journal, 15 May: p 648.

Ham C (1981) Policy-making in the National Health Service. London, Macmillan.

Ham C (1985) Health policy in Britain. 2nd edition. London, Macmillan.

Ham C and Hill M (1984) The policy process in the modern capitalist state. Brighton, Wheatsheaf Books.

Hanhan H J (1969) The development of the Scottish Office. In: Wolfe, J N (ed) Government and nationalism in Scotland. An enquiry by members of the University of Edinburgh. Edinburgh, Edinburgh University Press.

Hanhan H J (1985) Concluding remarks delivered at conference on the Scottish Office 1885–1985. University of Edinburgh, Edinburgh, 29–30 November.

Haywood H and Alaszewski A (1980) Crisis in the health service. London, Croom Helm.

Haywood S and Hunter D J (1982) Consultative processes in health policy in the United Kingdom: a view from the centre. Public Administration, 69, Summer, pp 143–162.

Health Advisory Service (1985) Annual report (June 1984–June 1985). Surrey, HAS.

Health Advisory Service and Social Work Service of the Welsh Office (1985a) Report on the joint visit to services provided for the elderly in the East Dyfed and Pembrokeshire health authorities. HAS/SWS(85)G416W, March, Wales.

Health Advisory Service and Social Work Service of the Welsh Office (1985b) Report on the joint visit to services provided for the elderly by the Gwent health authority, HAS/SWS(85)G427W, November, Wales.

Health Advisory Service and Social Work Service of the Welsh Office (1985c) Report on the joint visit to the services provided for the elderly in the South Glamorgan health authority and the social services department of the county of South Glamorgan. HAS/SWS(85)G24W, September, Wales.

Health Advisory Service and Social Work Service of the Welsh Office (1986) Report on the joint visit to services provided for mentally ill people by the Powys health authority and the social services department of the Powys county council, HAS/SWS(86)MI407W. March, Wales

Heclo H and Wildavsky, A (1981) The private government of public money. 2nd edition. London, Macmillan.

HM Treasury (1984) The government's expenditure plans 1984–85 to 1986–87. Cmnd 9143. London, HMSO.

Home Office (1946) Report on the committee on the care of children (Curtis report) Cmnd 6922. London, HMSO.

Hood C and Dunsire A (1981) Bureaumetrics. Aldershot, Gower.

House of Commons Committee of Public Accounts (1981) Financial control and accountability in the national health service. Seventeenth report, session 1980–81, HC 255. London, HMSO.

House of Commons Committee of Public Accounts (1982) Financial control and accountability in the national health service. Seventeenth report, session 1981–82, HC 375. London, HMSO.

House of Commons Committee of Public Accounts (1983a) Department of Health and Social Security. The joint financing of care by the National Health Service and local government. Eighth report, session 1982–83, HC 160. London, HMSO.

House of Commons Committee of Public Accounts (1983b) Minutes of evidence, Monday 24 January, session 1982–83, HC 160-i. London, HMSO.

House of Commons Social Services Committee (1980) The government's white papers on public expenditure: the social services. Third report, session 1979–80, HC 702-1. London, HMSO.

House of Commons Social Services Committee (1984) Public expenditure on the social services. Fourth report, session 1983–84, HC 395, London, HMSO.

House of Commons Social Services Committee (1985) Community care with special reference to adult mentally ill and mentally handicapped people. Second report, session 1984–85, HC 13–1. London, HMSO.

House of Commons Social Services Committee (1986) Public expenditure on the social services. Fourth report, session 1985–86, volumes I and II, HC 387–I and II. London, HMSO.

Hunter D J (1979) Decisions and resources within health authorities, Sociology of Health and Illness, 1, 1, June: pp 40–68.

Hunter D J (1980) Coping with uncertainty: policy and politics in the national health service. Chichester, John Wiley, Research Studies Press.

Hunter D J (1982) Organising for health: the national health service in the United Kingdom. Journal of Public Policy, 2, 3, August: pp 263–300.

Hunter D J (1983a) Centre-periphery relations in the national health service: facilitators or inhibitors of innovation? In: Young K (ed) National interests and local government. Joint Studies in Public Policy 7. London, Heinemann Educational: pp 133–161.

Hunter D J (1983b) Patterns of organisation for health: a systems overview of the national health service in the United Kingdom. In: Williamson A and Room G (eds) Health and welfare states of Britain: an inter-country comparison. London, Heinemann Educational: pp 56–88.

Hunter D J (1984) The lure of the organisational fix: re-reorganising the Scottish health service. In: McCrone D (ed) The Scottish government yearbook 1985. Edinburgh, Unit for the Study of Government: pp 230–257.

Hunter D J and Cantley C (1984) Exploring service variations in the care of the elderly. A voyage into the interior. In: Bromley D B (ed) Gerontology: social and behavioural perspectives. London, Croom Helm: pp 110–129.

Hunter D J, Cantley C and MacPherson I (1984) Psychogeriatric provision in Scotland: a review of research needs. Aberdeen, Unit for the Study of the Elderly, Department of Community Medicine, University of Aberdeen.

Hyde A (1986) Time for decision for principality, The Health Service Journal, 18 September: p 1220.

James J (1983) Some aspects of policy analysis and policy units in the health field. In Gray A and Jenkins B (eds) Policy analysis and evaluation in British government. London, Royal Institute of Public Administration: pp 57–60.

Jasp Team (1984) Joint approach to social policy: report of research funded by SSRC. University of Bath, University of Loughborough, Royal Institute of Public Administration.

Jones G (ed) (1980) New approaches to the study of central–local government relationships. Aldershot, Gower.

Karn V (1985) Housing. In Ranson S and others (eds) Between centre and locality. London, Allen and Unwin.

174

Keating M and Midwinter A (1983) The government of Scotland. Edinburgh, Mainstream.

Kellas J G (1975) The Scottish political system. 2nd edition. Cambridge, Cambridge University Press.

Kellas J G (1979) Central and local government. In: English J and Martin F M (eds) Social services in Scotland. Edinburgh, Scottish Academic Press: pp 5–17.

Kellas J G (1980) Modern Scotland. 2nd edition. London, Allen and Unwin.

Kellas J G and Madgwick P (1982) Territorial ministries: the Scottish and Welsh Offices. In: Madgwick P and Rose R (eds) The territorial dimension in UK politics. London Macmillan: pp 9–33.

King's Fund Centre (1980) An ordinary life. Project Paper 24. London. King's Fund Centre.

Klein R (1983a) The politics of the National Health Service. London, Longman.

Klein R (1983b) Strategies for comparative social policy research. In Williamson A and Room G (eds) Health and welfare states of Britain: an inter-country comparison. London, Heinemann Educational: pp 13–25.

Klein R (1985) Health policy 1979–83: the retreat from ideology? In: Jackson P (ed) Implementing government policy initiatives: the Thatcher administration 1979–83. London, Royal Institute of Public Administration: pp 189–207.

Laing W (1985) Private health care 1985. London, Office of Health Economics.

Leary W D (1983) Planning – the Lothian approach. Hospital and Health Services Review, 79, 6, November: pp 280–285.

Lipsky M (1978) Standing the study of public policy implementation on its head. In: Burnham W D and Weinberg M W (eds) American politics and public policy. Cambridge, MA, MIT Press: pp 391–402.

McGirr E M (1984) Planning health care in Scotland. British Medical Journal, 289, 22 September: pp 776–8.

McGuire, A (1985) Scotland v England. THS Health Summary, II, XI, November: p 1.

McKeganey N P and Hunter D J (1986) 'Only connect . . . ': tightrope walking and joint working in the care of the elderly. Policy and Politics, 14, 3: pp 335–360

Mackintosh J P (1976) The problems of devolution – the Scottish case. In Griffiths, J A G (ed) From policy to administration. London, Allen and Unwin.

Madgwick P and James M (1980) The network of consultative government in Wales. In: Jones, G (ed) New approaches to the study of central–local government relations. Aldershot, Gower: pp 101–115.

Madgwick P and Rose R (1982) Introduction. In: Madgwick P and Rose R (eds) The territoral dimension in UK politics. London, Macmillan: pp 1–6.

Madgwick P and Rose R (eds) (1982) The territorial dimension in UK politics. London, Macmillan.

Martin F M (1984) Between the acts. Community mental health services 1959–1983. London, The Nuffield Provincial Hospitals Trust.

Means R and Smith R (1985) The development of welfare services for elderly people. London, Croom Helm.

Ministry of Health (1956) Report of the committee of enquiry into the cost of the National Health Service (Chairman, C W Guillebaud) Cmd 9663. London, HMSO.

Ministry of Health (1963) Health and welfare: the development of community care. Plans for the health and welfare services of the local authorities in England and Wales. Cmnd 1973. London, HMSO.

Ministry of Health (1966) The hospital building programme: a revision of the hospital plan for England and Wales. Cmnd 3000. London, HMSO.

Moyes W (1985) Scrutiny of the central advisory service (social work services). Report to the Minister for Home Affairs Health and Social Work. Edinburgh, Scottish Office.

Murray N (1986) DHSS: you're partners now. Social Services Insight, May 3–10: pp 6–7.

Nairne Sir P (1983) Managing the DHSS elephant: reflections on a giant department. Political Quarterly, 54, 3, July–September: pp 243–56.

Nairne P (1985) Managing the National Health Service. British Medical Journal, 291, 13 July: pp 121–4.

National Association of Health Authorities (1982) Index of joint finance schemes. Birmingham, NAHA.

Nicholls R M (1981) Pivots and links in the National Health Service: some ways of improving centre-periphery co-ordination. London, Linkage Six, Centre for Organisational and Operational Research: pp 12–18.

North Western Regional Health Authority (1982) Services for people who are mentally handicapped: a model district service. Manchester, North Western Regional Health Authority.

Norton A and Rogers S (1981) The health service and local government services. Can they work together to meet the needs of the elderly and of other disadvantaged groups? Why is collaboration a problem? In: McLachlan G (ed) Matters of moment. London, OUP for the Nuffield Provincial Hospitals Trust: pp 107–152.

Outer Circle Policy Unit (1980) Health first: a comment on 'patients first'. London, OCPU.

Owen D (1979) Reflections on the Royal Commission. The Trevor Lloyd Hughes Memorial Lecture, 25 October (unpublished mimeo).

Page E (1980) Why should central-local relations in Scotland be different from those in England?. In: Jones, G (ed) New approaches to the study of central-local government relations. Aldershot, Gower: pp 84–99.

Parker J (1965) Local health and welfare services. London, Allen and Unwin.

Parliament (1976) Fit for the future: report of the committee on child health services (Chairman, S D M Court) Cmnd 6684. London, HMSO.

Parliament (1979) Report of the committee of inquiry into mental handicap nursing and care (Chairman, Peggy Jay) Cmnd 7468. London, HMSO.

Parry R (1981) Scotland as a laboratory for public administration. Paper prepared for 6th annual conference of the PSA UK Politics Work Group, Glasgow, September

Parry R (1985) The Scottish Office and social policy. Paper delivered at conference on the Scottish Office 1885–1985. Edinburgh, University of Edinburgh, 29–30 November.

Ranson S (1984) Towards a tertiary tripartism: new codes of social control and the 17+. In: Broadfoot P (ed) Selection, certification and control. London, Falmer Press.

Ranson S, Jones G and Walsh K(eds) (1985) Between centre and locality. London, Allen and Unwin.

Regan D (1977) Local government and education. London, Allen and Unwin.

Regional Chairmen (1976) Enquiry into the working of the DHSS in relation to regional health authorities. London, DHSS.

Rhodes R A W, Hardy B and Pudney K (1983) Constraints on the national community of local government: members, 'other governments' and policy communities. Discussion paper No 6. Essex, Department of Government, University of Essex.

Rhodes R A W and Midwinter A F (1980) Corporate management: the new conventional wisdom in British local government. Studies in public policy no 59. Glasgow, Centre for the Study of Public Policy, University of Strathclyde.

Rodgers B with Doron A and Jones M (1979) The study of social policy: a comparative approach. London, Allen and Unwin.

Royal Commission on the Constitution (1973) Volume 1, Report. Cmnd 5460. London, HMSO.

Royal Commission on the National Health Service (1978) The working of the National Health Service. Research paper no 1. London, HMSO.

Royal Commission on the National Health Service (1979) Report. Cmnd 7615. London, HMSO.

Royal Institute of Public Administration (1981) Care in the community: a response. A memorandum prepared for submission to the DHSS. London, RIPA (mimeo).

Scottish Action on Dementia (1986) An analysis of responses to the Scottish Action on Dementia policy document 'Dementia in Scotland: priorities for care, strategies for change'. Edinburgh. Scottish Action on Dementia.

Scottish Home and Health Department (1966) Administrative practice of hospital boards in Scotland (Chairman, W M Farquharson-Lang) Edinburgh, HMSO.

Scottish Home and Health Department (1976) The health service in Scotland: the way ahead. Edinburgh, HMSO.

Scottish Home and Health Department (1977) Working party on relationships between health boards and local authorities: report. Edinburgh, SHHD.

Scottish Home and Health Department (1980a) Joint planning and support financing arrangements. NHS circular no 1980(GEN)5. Edinburgh, SHHD.

Scottish Home and Health Department (1980b) Scottish health authorities priorities for the eighties. Edinburgh, HMSO.

Scottish Home and Health Department (1981) Monitoring of progress towards implementing the SHAPE priorities. NHS circular no 1981 (GEN)46. Edinburgh, SHHD.

Scottish Home and Health Department (1983) Structure and management of the NHS in Scotland: abolition of district level of management. NHS circular no 1983(GEN)27. Edinburgh, SHHD.

Scottish Home and Health Department (1984) The general management function in the NHS in Scotland: proposals for discussion. Edinburgh, SHHD.

Scottish Home and Health Department (1985) General management in the Scottish health service: implementation – the first steps. NHS circular no 1985(GEN)4. Edinburgh, SHHD.

Scottish Home and Health Department (1986a) General management in the Scottish health service: application to units. Report by Coopers and Lybrand Associates. Edinburgh, SHHD.

Scottish Home and Health Department (1986b) General management in the Scottish health service: general management at unit level and the development of senior management structures. NHS circular no 1986(GEN)20. Edinburgh, SHHD.

Scottish Home and Health Department (1986c) SHAPE monitoring and strategic planning: second round. SHHD/DGM18(1986)13. Edinburgh, SHHD.

Scottish Home and Health Department and Scottish Education Department (1972) Services for the mentally handicapped. Edinburgh, SHHD.

Scottish Home and Health Department and Scottish Education Department (1979) A better life: report on services for the mentally handicapped in Scotland. Edinburgh, HMSO.

Scottish Home and Health Department and Scottish Education Department (1985) Mental health in focus: report on the mental health services for adults in Scotland. Edinburgh, HMSO.

Scottish Office (1985) Community care: joint planning and support finance. NHS 1985(GEN)18, SW5/1985, SDD15/1985, SED1127/1985. Edinburgh, Scottish Office.

Smart C (1986) A marriage of two minds. Community Care, April 24: pp 20–21.

Smith G (1983) The 'auld enemy': comparing different systems for delivering the personal social services and juvenile justice in Great Britain. In Williamson, A and Room, G (eds) Health and welfare states of Britain: an inter-country comparison. London, Heinemann Educational: pp 107–129.

Social Science and Research Council (1979) Central–local government relationships. Report of an SSRC Panel to the Research Initiatives Board. London, SSRC.

Stewart J D (1977) Have the Scots a lesson to teach? Municipal Journal, 19 January.

Stowe, Sir K (1984) Sorting out lines of accountability. Health and Social Service Journal, June 14: p 698.

Tinker A (1984) Staying at home: helping elderly people. London, HMSO.

The Unemployed Voluntary Action Fund (1986) Report of the first four years 1982–1986. London, Carnegie, United Kingdom Trust.

University of Aberdeen/Loughborough University (1986) Survey of arrangements for health and local authority collaboration in Scotland: analysis of responses. Aberdeen, Department of Community Medicine, University of Aberdeen (mimeo).

Webb A and Wistow G (1982) The personal social services: planning, incrementalism or systematic social planning? In: Walker A (ed) Public expenditure and social policy: an examination of social spending and priorities. London, Heinemann Educational: pp 137–164.

Webb A and Wistow G (1985) The personal social services. In: Ranson S and others (eds) Between centre and locality. London, Allen and Unwin.

Webb A and Wistow G (1986) Planning, need and scarcity: essays on the personal social services. London, Allen and Unwin.

179

Webb A and Wistow G (1987) Social work, social care and social planning: the personal social services since Seebohm. London, Longman.

Welsh Office (1975) Health service planning: a short guide. Health and Social Work Department. Cardiff, Welsh Office.

Welsh Office (1976) Proposed all-Wales policies and priorities for the planning and provision of health and personal social services from 1976/77 to 1979/80. A consultative document. Cardiff, Welsh Office.

Welsh Office (1977) Joint planning–health and local authorities joint financing of personal social services projects. WHC(77)21. Cardiff, Welsh Office.

Welsh Office (1978) Joint financing of personal social services projects: WHC(78)13. Welsh Office circular 51/78. Cardiff, Welsh Office.

Welsh Office (1979) Joint financing of personal social services projects: 1979/80. WHC(79)1. Welsh Office circular 14/79. Cardiff, Welsh Office.

Welsh Office (1980) The structure and management of the NHS in Wales. Cardiff, HMSO.

Welsh Office (1981) Care in the Community. A consultative document on moving resources for care in Wales. Cardiff, Welsh Office.

Welsh Office (1982) Report of the all-Wales working party on services for mentally handicapped people. Cardiff, Welsh Office.

Welsh Office (1983a) All Wales strategy for the development of services for mentally handicapped people. Cardiff, Welsh Office.

Welsh Office (1983b) Health and social services development: 'care in the community' – services for people who are mentally handicapped, mentally ill, elderly or physically handicapped. Welsh Office circular 15/83. Cardiff, Welsh Office.

Welsh Office (1984a) The NHS management inquiry report – implementation in Wales. Welsh Office circular WHC(84)15. Cardiff, Welsh Office.

Welsh Office (1984b) The NHS management inquiry report – implementation in Wales. Essential elements of the job descriptions of district health authority CAMOs, CANOs and treasurers. Welsh Office circular WHC(84)22. Cardiff, Welsh Office.

Welsh Office (1985a) All Wales mental handicap strategy. County Monitoring Reports. Cardiff, Welsh Office.

Welsh Office (1985b) Policies and priorities for health services in Wales. Cardiff, Welsh Office.

Welsh Office (1985c) Reorganisation of health, housing and social affairs responsibilities within the Welsh Office. Welsh Office circular WHC(85)24. Cardiff, Welsh Office.

Westland P (1981) The year of the voluntary organisation. Community Care, 19 November: pp 14–15.

Williamson A and Room G (eds) (1983) Health and welfare states of Britain: an inter-country comparison. London, Heinemann Educational.

Wiseman C (1979) Policy making in the Scottish health services at national level, In: Drucker N and Drucker H M (eds) The Scottish government yearbook 1980. Edinburgh, Paul Harris: pp 135–160.

Wistow G (1980) Inter-organisational relationships: the National Health Service. Town Planning Review, 51, 3: pp 302–305.

Wistow G (1982) Collaboration between health and local authorities: why is it necessary? Social Policy and Administration, 16, 1: pp 44–62.

Wistow G (1983) Joint finance and community care: have the incentives worked? Public Money, 3, 2: pp 33–37.

Wistow G (1985) Community care for the mentally handicapped: disappointing progress. In: Harrison A and Gretton J (eds) Health care UK 1985. London, Chartered Institute of Public Finance and Accountancy: pp 69–78.

Wistow G (1986) Increasing private provision of social care: implications for policy. In: Lewis R and others (eds) Care and control: social services and the private sector. London, Policy Studies Institute.

Wistow G (1987) Collaboration between health and local authorities: lessons and prospects. In: Wistow G and Brooks T (eds) Joint planning and joint management. London, Royal Institute of Public Administration (forthcoming).

Wistow G and Fuller S (1983) Joint planning in perspective: the NAHA survey of collaboration 1976–1982. Loughborough and Birmingham, Centre for Research in Social Policy and National Association of Health Authorities.

Wistow G and Fuller S (1986) Collaboration since restructuring: the 1984 survey of joint planning and joint finance. Loughborough and Birmingham, Centre for Research in Social Policy and National Association of Health Authorities.

Wistow G and Hardy B (1986) Transferring care: can financial incentives work? In: Harrison A and Gretton J (eds) Health care UK 1986. London, Chartered Institute of Public Finance and Accountancy: pp 103–110; and in Public Money, December 1985: pp 31–36.

Wistow G and Head S (1981) Pump-priming programme. Health and Social Service Journal, 3 July: pp 806–807.

Wistow G and Webb A (1980) Patients first: one step backwards for collaboration? In: Webb A and Wistow G (1986) Planning, need and scarcity: essays on the personal social services. London, Allen and Unwin.

Wistow G and Wray K (1986) CMHTs, service delivery and service development: the Nottinghamshire approach. In: Grant G, Humphreys S and McGrath M (eds) Community mental handicap teams: theory and practice. Kidderminster, British Institute of Mental Handicap.

181

Wolfenberger W (1972) The principle of normalisation in human services. Toronto, National Institute on Mental Retardation.

Working Group on Joint Planning (1985) Progress in partnership. London, DHSS.